Program Handbook
for
Women's Ministries

Program Handbook for Women's Ministries
You Asked for It!

by
Berniece Garsee

Beacon Hill Press of Kansas City
Kansas City, Missouri

Copyright 1984
Beacon Hill Press of Kansas City

ISBN: 0-8341-0924-7

Printed in the
United States of America

10 9 8 7 6 5 4 3 2 1

Contents

Preface

When my pastor husband and our family moved to Boise in 1976, I felt the pull to begin working with ladies' ministries. Even as a pastor's wife it was all new to me—I am a first grade schoolteacher! As we began, however, I remember that my friend Robbie said to me, "Berniece, if God is in it, you don't have to push. The Holy Spirit will lead." Since that time we have been amazed to see what God has done in the lives of our ladies and in our church.

One day last spring I ate lunch with Faye Stowe who was visiting as our Ladies' Retreat speaker. During our conversation she asked me to compile a book on programming for Ladies' Ministries. With some fear I accepted the challenge.

Since then I have traveled back in time to relive each of these special happenings. For me, it has been a Spirit-directed journey. This book is intended as a compilation of ideas for you to adapt to your ministry situation. Use what you can and file the rest away. Because you asked for these ideas, concepts, and processes, I am praying we will be better co-laborers with God in the adventure of ladies' ministries.

Berniece Garsee
Boise, Idaho
1984

Acknowledgments

Approximately 60 percent of this book is comprised of the original material used in our ministry at First Church of the Nazarene, Boise, Idaho.

Thank you to all my partners in Women's Ministries who collectively contributed the other 40 percent. The original manuscript included contributions that do not appear in the book due to lack of space, but the names of all contributors are included here to thank them equally for their willingness to share.

Pam Alexander
Virna Birkey
Britta Bridges
Dorothy Cantrell
Sheila Cantrell
Lena Cremeens
Lynn Cross
Lynn Deakins
Ruth Green
Roberta Halley
Raedean Henecke
Ruth Human

Kitty Jones
Wilda Majors
Patti McElrath
Marcia L. Mitchell
Marie Price
Alberta Rodes
Wilma Shaw
Ginger Shingler
Dee Smith
Gayla Stowe
Carol Stueckle
Juanita Thomas
Paulette Woods

*Making It Happen
at Boise First Church*

Our women's ministries program at Boise First Church of the Nazarene has two goals:

1. To encourage deeper relationships and spiritual growth for women in our church.

2. To influence ladies in the community to accept Jesus Christ as their personal Savior.

We work toward these goals through four basic programs. The starting point was our Ladies' Fellowship Bible Study. A committee was chosen to work out plans and Bible topics for each weekly meeting. After that beginning, three other groups were formed: Night Ladies' Bible Study, 3-D Groups (Diet, Discipline, and Discipleship), and Retreats.

From the chairmen of these groups, an executive committee was formed. Other members could be added to the Executive Committee as needed to improve effectiveness.

The following is a diagram of the organizational chart we are working toward:

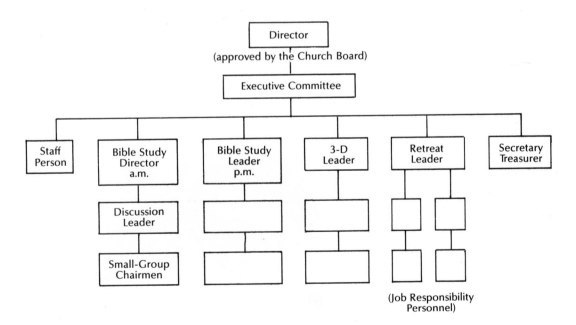

The Executive Committee endeavors to accomplish two things as it meets each month:

1. Each member reports to the other members of the committee what is happening in her particular area.

2. The committee plans special events for the entire year. Other ladies outside the

committee are selected from questionnaires and sign-up sheets, or are personally recruited for specific tasks.

Planning for One Year

The course of planning for one particular year in our ministry begins in the July, August, and September meetings of the Executive Committee. The specific agenda for these meetings progresses from month to month, but by the third committee meeting the following goals should have been accomplished:

1. Make general plans for special events for the entire year (event, place, speaker, date, mistress of ceremonies). Check the church calendar so there will be no conflicts with other activities.

2. Coordinate plans and studies for weekly activities. Each group meets separately to plan its particular activities, but the committee chairman reports to the executive group.

3. Plan in detail the first special event for the Fall Kick-off. The date and speaker should be confirmed six months ahead of time.

4. Plan the yearly booklet or brochure, which is to be given to each lady at the first activity. (See sample from Boise First Church, appendix, page 76.) Even though all details are not complete, this helps to create excitement and enthusiasm for the upcoming year.

5. Begin publishing a monthly newsletter. Create your own logo, color, and style. (This is an effective way to coordinate all aspects of your ministry to women and keep the ladies informed.)

The preceding plan and committee structuring worked well for Boise First. We offer it only as a suggested procedure to stimulate your thinking. Chapter 1 will give you some concrete guidelines for your planning, which are adaptable to any ministry situation.

1

The Planning Process for Special Events

JOB RESPONSIBILITIES

Planning Meetings
Job Assignments
Publicity
Registration
Food
Table Service
Cleanup

RETREAT PLANNING

Six Months Before
Three Months Before
One Month Before
Two Weeks Before
Weekend of Retreat
After Retreat

ON-SITE COORDINATION

Welcome
Hostesses
Group Dynamics
Speaker

FOLLOW-UP

Questionnaires
Evaluation Forms
Information Sheets for New Ladies
Information Sheets for Regular Attenders

1 The Planning Process for Special Events

Thorough and detailed planning for any event is extremely important. It involves people, improves motivation, and guarantees a more relaxed and effective event. Following are some general guidelines to improve your planning strategy.

JOB RESPONSIBILITIES

Planning Meetings

Sometimes it will be difficult for your chairman to get every member of the Executive Committee present for the planning sessions. To expedite communication, choose a secretary and send minutes to each member for inclusion in their special "committee" notebook. This will prevent absences from breaking the continuity of your effort.

If you are having monthly meetings, they may be scheduled the same day each month. Or if this isn't possible, you may find it best to include the establishment of future meeting dates as a part of the agenda for each meeting. It will not be necesary, then, for the chairman to make personal calls to arrange meeting times. Also, the responsibility to attend is placed directly upon the members.

Job Assignments

These will differ with each occasion. Refer to the appendix: Planning Check List, page 75, or the Planning Accountability Sheet, page 77.

Publicity

A lot of good publicity is vitally important to bring your women together in Ladies' Ministries. Every lady in the congregation should feel she is missing out if she does not participate. Exciting publicity can overcome negativism and make huge successes out of programs that were previously failures.

A. *For any event . . .*
1. Put the date on the church calendar immediately. (Chairman usually does this.)
2. Put notices in the midweek bulletin, beginning several weeks before event.
3. Put inserts in the Sunday bulletins for several Sundays.
4. Ask the pastor to announce the event from the pulpit several weeks in advance.
5. Ask the pastor to get feedback from Friendship and Worship cards for several consecutive weeks. (Circle "L" on Friendship and Wor-

ship card indicating interest in ladies events.)

6. Recruit Ladies' Fellowship support. (Morning Bible Study group, word of mouth, prayer, attendance, involvement.)
7. Make posters and design a bulletin board announcement.
8. If you are selling tickets and tables are set up in the foyer, announce from the pulpit (and also in Sunday bulletins) *who* is sitting at the table.
9. Divide the names from your church directory for the committee to call. Give a personal invitation. (Each calling committee member should have a list of those who have already signed up.)

B. *For retreats . . .*

In addition to the general ideas listed above,

1. Ask the retreat chairman or publicity person to announce the retreat from the pulpit.
2. Ask the pastor to interview the retreat chairman.
3. If the retreat is expensive, put inserts in the Sunday bulletins beginning six months ahead on the first Sunday of each month. Use this to offer a time payment plan.
4. Have a representative in each Sunday School class who is excited about the retreat promote it. Take the names of those interested. Encourage them to buy a ticket either from representative or in the foyer.
5. Write a skit to be given on Sunday morning or evening, two or three weeks prior to the retreat. (Refer to sample skit following.)
6. If your speaker has written books, have them available for purchase.
7. To undergird your publicity, make a chart for your private use (See Sample Suggestion below) listing all names with appropriate information. Pray over these specifically.

Retreat			
Name	Plan to Attend? Yes No	If No, Reason Given	Prayer Concerns

C. *For outreach events, additional publicity . . .*

1. Place posters in the church, in Christian bookstores, in businesses, etc.
2. Put a spot announcement on a Christian radio station, asking people to call the church office for reservations.
3. Place ads in local newspapers.
4. Send a packet including a letter, poster, and free ticket to your area ministers' wives.

Sample Publicity Skit for Ladies' Retreat

SCENE:

Jim enters pushing a grocery cart, accompanied by three-year-old twin boys and five-year-old daughter, Dana. The only thing he picks up are two large boxes labeled "Hot Dogs."

DANA: That's not the kind Mommy buys.

JIM: Well, Mommy's *(pause)* not here.

(Darrell enters pushing empty shopping cart, greets Jim, looks in shopping cart.)

DARRELL: A little heavy on the hot dogs, aren't ya, Jim?

JIM: Well, you know, you can do so much with them—like weiners and eggs for breakfast, hot dogs for lunch, chili dogs for dinner, or if the kids really want to go for it, we'll broil tube steaks. I like to mix it up a bit. I've got enough weiners here to last through the whole Ladies' Retreat.

DARRELL: The retreat only goes from Friday evening through Saturday afternoon.

JIM: That's odd. Patti said she would be gone all week! *(pause)* How are you getting along for meals?

DARRELL: Real good! Last night we had beef jerky, carrot sticks, and saltine crackers with jelly beans for dessert. A little something from each of the basic food groups, you know.

JIM: You should have called! If we had known you were making a full course dinner, we'd have come over.

DARRELL: Yeah, you could have helped me clean up the kitchen. What a disaster! Say, I wonder how our wives are doing without us?

JIM: Oh, they're probably hurting.

DARRELL: I understand they're having a special speaker at the Ladies' Retreat—some guy named Lee Hazel?

JIM: No. That's Hazel Lee.

DARRELL: Strange name for a guy.

JIM: No, he's a she, a pastor's wife from Pasadena, California.

DARRELL: Oh, the little old lady from Pasadena! Well, with a name like Hazel Lee, she's got to be good.

JIM: Careful—you never know who might be listening. *(looking at wallet)* Do you have some money I can borrow to pay for these groceries? I could have sworn I had $35.00 in my wallet.

DARRELL: Really, that's funny. The Ladies' Retreat cost exactly $35.00. I think I've got some money here you can use.

JIM: Great. *(while Darrell gets wallet)* By the way, how's the baby doing?

DARRELL: Oh, the baby! Jim, I forgot to bring the baby! *(very hurriedly now)* Well, Jim, it's been nice talking with you. I've got to get home right away!

JIM *(reaching for money, looks in wallet and then at child)*: Dana, do you have any money?

KIDS: Daddy, I'm hungry.

JIM *(to audience)*: As you can see . . . a few minor kinks . . . no major problems . . . so, ladies, if you want to go to the retreat, you've got nothing to worry about.

Registration

(The chairman may want to help with this responsibility.) Set up tables in the foyer several consecutive Sundays before the event.

1. Have a sign-up sheet and sell tickets. If this is a retreat, there should be a choice of roommates.
2. Distribute information sheet (for retreats only). This answers all questions concerning the retreat and should be given out at the same time the ladies sign up.
3. Keep financial records.
4. Bank money (if you have a separate account).
5. Pay bills, speaker, and reimburse committee members for all expenses.
6. Make the following arrangements with place in which the event is to be held:
   —estimated number to attend
   —setting . . . type of tables, podium, public address system, piano, tablecloths, napkins
   —room reservations (for retreats)
   —menu selections (the committee will have made some of these decisions previously)
7. Forty-five minutes before the event is to begin, sit at entry table (with name tag committee member)
   —to take tickets
   —to collect any outstanding money
   —to sign up ladies who haven't preregistered
   —to get a count of all ladies present

Food

If your ladies are preparing the food for the event, a person will need to be in charge. After the committee has decided on the menu, the food chairman will:

1. Ask various ladies to prepare a dish or bring a certain food item.
2. Send a letter to those ladies with information notifying them of the time the food is needed and include the recipe they are to prepare.
3. Ask some ladies to work in the kitchen before and during the meal.

Table Service

Find a different crew to serve the ladies and wait on tables during the meal. Teens or men are usually glad to do this. If serving buffet style, hostesses may be responsible for refilling drinks.

Cleanup

The chairman is responsible for her own kitchen cleanup crew. One person from each table (these can also be the hostesses) should bring the dishes into the kitchen and remove the tablecloths. These hostesses may be asked ahead of time or the mistress of ceremonies can choose them at the event.

RETREAT PLANNING

Six Months Before

1. Decide if this will be: a one-night retreat within the community; a weekend retreat with food provided; a weekend retreat with ladies providing the food; or your own new idea.
2. Set a date and put on church calendar as soon as possible.
3. Select speaker, call, and confirm with letter.
4. Choose theme; write to tell speaker.
5. Reserve the location. Arrange for approximate number of rooms and meeting rooms. Ask if payment can be made in a lump sum the last day of the retreat.
6. After determining all the above, estimate your attendance. Divide this number into hotel costs, plus food costs, plus speaker expense and honorarium. If you skimp too much, someone will end up in the red. Overestimate and have some creative way to use the excess money—perhaps a fund for ladies who can't afford to attend the next retreat.

Three Months Before

1. Begin distributing and collecting registration forms.
2. Assign job responsibilities:
   —Favors
   —Door Prizes
   —Programs
   —Name Tags
   —Posters
   —Centerpieces
   —Games
   —Entertainment (Will you need a piano? Let the retreat facility know.)
3. Write speaker to tell her you are praying for her.
4. Find teenagers or others in the church who will baby-sit for attendees.

One Month Before

1. Meet to check progress on job responsibilities.
2. Increase publicity to let ladies know it's almost registration deadline.
3. Select menu.

Two Weeks Before

1. Keep praying.
2. Give hotel final rooming list (women's names listed by room) and keep a copy.
3. Tell latecomers that if someone cancels you will call or if they can get a roommate to come, you'll try to reserve another room.
4. Tell cancellations they will need to sell their spot. You can't refund money at this point because you've guaranteed to the hotel.

5. Send each attendee a letter of encouragement and an information sheet with directions.

Weekend of Retreat
1. Pray.
2. Make speaker comfortable.
3. Greet ladies at the entrance.
4. Start all meetings on time. Be sensitive to the ladies' fatigue and to their moods.

After Retreat
1. Pay retreat facility and all expenses.
2. Thank speaker, hotel, committee members, and attendees.
3. Thank your husband and family.
4. Thank the Lord.

ON-SITE COORDINATION

The people are arriving. It's the moment of truth. What happens in the next few hours will determine whether your ladies come back next time and whether they'll be excited about bringing a friend. Depend on the Holy Spirit and use these three elements for success: organization, coordination, and communication.

Welcome Center
Set up an entry table where committee members give name tags, take money, or perform their jobs for that particular occasion. Decorate the table to say "Welcome, we're glad you're here."

Hostesses
Hostesses should have hostess tags or ribbons on their name tags. (If the occasion is in the fellowship hall, it's nice to have a punch table with a hostess serving.) Ask the hostesses to come early to find their tables, to greet, to welcome, and to create an atmosphere of warmth. They should befriend any lady who seems to be alone. Hostesses should meet with emcee earlier to get instructions for small-group dynamics during the evening.

Group Dynamics
(Koinonia Fellowship)—The chairman usually plans this.

Special food, special speaker, and special program do not necessarily lead to New Testament koinonia fellowship. That only happens in Spirit-anointed small-group interaction.

Some have commented they do not like small-group sharing because it is "too personal," "too negative," or "not confidential." This feeling may be overcome through positive interaction—by consistently asking nonthreatening (not too personal) questions, by seeing answers to prayer, and in general by bearing each others burdens and so fulfilling the law of Christ.

Three types of small groups are effective in the ministries discussed in this book. You may have one or all of them in a given schedule.

1. *Sharing at your table* (planned interaction led by hostesses). Some guidelines for "Getting to know one another" are:
   —Make introductions.
   —Lead planned interaction.
   —Don't go around the circle if the question is too personal.
   —Never pray around the circle. Some people may be shy, you may have new Christians, and you hope to have unbelievers present.
   —Be aware of all ladies—include everyone.

2. *Sharing in small groups* (discussion led by hostess in a separate location). Some guidelines for "Getting to know the Word" are:
   —Get acquainted. Share name, family, occupation, one good happening in your life, etc.
   —Read Scripture together.
   —Share insights and applications to your life.
   —Share responses to planned interaction questions.
   —Share special concerns.
   —Pray for one another—open conversational prayer.

3. *Sharing in prayer cells* (personal sharing, led by hostesses). Some guidelines for "Getting to know God" are:
   —Share blessings, insights, needs, and prayer.
   —Begin on positive note; for example: Blessing. What good thing is happening in your life?
   —Lead the discussion. Don't let any one person take over.
   —Share what the Lord has been saying to you in your daily quiet time.
   —Share recent answers to prayer and urgent requests.
   —Use conversational prayer or leader pray.
   —Dismiss on a positive note.

Sometimes small groups continue to meet after the event is over because they feel the need to share in each other's lives for prayer and encouragement.

The Speaker

Specifically, these guidelines are for retreats, but they can be adapted.

1. A year or more in advance the committee should choose the speaker—go for the best.
2. Contact the person immediately and confirm the date.
3. As soon as the committee has decided on the theme, notify the speaker. At least two months in advance will give time for the messages to fit the program.
4. Send the speaker a copy of the program, including the number of times she will be used and the time allotments for each.
5. Let your guest know the weather expected, the most practical attire to wear, the recreational facilities available, and the number of people registered.

6. Confirm arrival times, transportation provisions, and housing arrangements. Everything that will add to the ease, comfort, and warmth of the speaker will make for a better retreat.

7. Once she's here, give her . . .
   —flowers or fruit (goodies) in the room
   —a note of welcome
   —a program and a name tag
   —any special instructions
   —a moment to freshen up before the start of the retreat
   —a time to be alone with the Lord

8. Be courteous . . .
   —The pastor's wife or committee chairman should escort the guest to the first gathering.
   —If committee chairman is busy with final preparations, assign someone to be with the guest.
   —Give the speaker a time to meet others, but do not leave her alone—it becomes awkward.
   —Familiarize the speaker with the area and people as much as possible.
   —At the close of the retreat, give the speaker an appropriate memento of the occasion.

FOLLOW-UP

Printed follow-up tools and an evaluation meeting by the committee will help you to gauge the effectiveness of your event. Use them to assess the current needs of the ladies in your group and to improve planning for the future.

Questionnaire

A questionnaire can be used effectively at the Fall Kick-off Event or perhaps in church on a Sunday morning. Place the questionnaire inside the morning bulletin and ask the ladies to complete them during Sunday School. Give a reminder from the pulpit. (See Appendix, pages 78-79, 81.)

Evaluation forms

Distribute these during an event, usually close to the end, to evaluate your ministry. Keep in mind your purpose for each event. Did you accomplish your goals? Are you reaching new ladies? (See Appendix, page 80.)

Information Sheets for new ladies

You have a list of all ladies who preregistered for your special event. In some cases, you may have personal information on a 3″ x 5″ card the ladies turned in.

Write a letter to all new ladies, thanking them for coming and inviting them to become a part of the total program. Include a brochure, yearly booklet, or newsletter. In some instances a personal visit would be worthwhile.

As new ladies visit your church, have a plan to share information with them about Ladies' Ministries.

Information Sheets for regular attenders

Send a follow-up letter thanking your own ladies for coming. Ask for names of, and information about, their friends.

Write an article in the ladies' newsletter describing the "Afterglow" of an exciting event. Use it to create enthusiasm for upcoming events.

2

Ideas for Special Events

BANQUETS

Transfigured
Sharing the Treasure
Doorways and Discoveries
The Family
Granny's Attic
Outer Splendor
Secret Pals

RETREATS

Be Ye Transformed
Reflections of His Image

Make Love Your Aim
Doorways and Discoveries
Walk Worthy
Women Fashioned by God
Living to Serve
Hats off to You
Growing in Christ

SEASONAL ACTIVITIES

Valentine's Day
Mother's Day
Christmas

2 Ideas for Special Events

Normally, the only special events in women's ministries that require extensive planning fall into one of three categories: banquets (or teas, luncheons, etc.), retreats (one- or two-day), and seasonal activities (Christmas, Mother's Day, etc.). This chapter will help you plan for these—it is a compilation of suggested themes and specifics for coordinating them to your particular event.

Sample formats are at the beginning of the sections "Banquets" and "Retreats." These include an agenda for a banquet or retreat, plus specific planning details. Following the sample are numerous variations —themes and suggestions for special features, games, centerpieces, and small-group interaction activities.

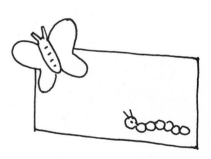

BANQUETS
(detailed agenda)

Theme: TRANSFIGURED
Scripture: Rom. 12:2
Welcome: 7 p.m.
Get Acquainted: Choose a game from Chapter 3
Dinner: Salad Buffet. Serve cafeteria style. Call tables by number.
Music: "What a Difference He Makes in My Life"
Introduction of Theme:

"The theme 'Transfiguration' is from the book *Lord, Change Me,* by Evelyn Christensen.

"She quotes Rom. 12:2—'Be not conformed to this world: but be ye transformed by the renewing of your mind . . .' Transformed— same word as Christ's 'Transfigured.' Did God want me changed as dramatically as Christ was on the Mount of Transfiguration when His face shone as the sun and His raiment was as white as the light? Then I wrote 'changed—from worm to butterfly.'"

Introduction to Speaker:
Prayer and Share: (led by hostesses at each table after speaker concludes)

1. What impressed you about the message tonight?
2. In what area of your life are you in the process of becoming transformed?
   Hostesses pray.

Chorus: "Little by Little He's Changing Me"

Decorations:

Colors—Gold and white

Centerpiece: Use small votive candles in glass snifters, with a butterfly taped to the base. To make butterfly, use black construction paper and cut out inside of wings. Glue colored tissue paper in cutout part.

To add caterpillars, paint an upside down egg carton with green tempera paint. Use black Magic Marker for face, black chenille wire for antennae.

Name Tags: Gold butterflies or caterpillars

Food: A salad dinner on the church campus is one of the easiest "Ladies' Night Out" events. Ask each lady to bring a salad. The planning committee should bring rolls and butter.

Greeters: Have selected ladies take the salads as they come in. This will alleviate confusion in the kitchen.

Follow-up: The hostesses should give the names of any new ladies to the chairman. The committee then arranges a follow-up.

Children: Nursery provided

Variations on Banquet Themes

Theme: SHARING THE TREASURE

Scripture: 2 Cor. 4:7 (TLB)

Get Acquainted: "The treasure of personality" (oral responses at table)
1. What treasure do you have in your purse that probably no one else in the room has?
2. Share a treasure of one of your most valued achievements.
3. Share a treasured memory of a particular person who has influenced your life.

Centerpiece: Arrange daisies in small wooden chests you have collected beforehand. Use yellow candles to accent.

Name Tags/Hostess Tags: Treasure chests mimeographed on yellow construction paper.

Theme: DOORWAYS AND DISCOVERIES

Scripture: Rev. 3:8

Get Acquainted: Discovering each other (oral responses at table. Limit to 10 minutes.)
1. What is the most unusual thing your friend would discover in your purse?
2. What is the most fulfilling discovery that you made in the last 12 months?
3. What new door do you see opening for you in your life in the next 12 months?

Special Feature: Discover through reading.

Have someone review books from church library or local Christian bookstore. Set up a book table for browsing before and after the banquet.

Name Tags: Make welcome mats out of construction paper.

Theme: THE FAMILY

Decorations: One lady acts as hostess for each table. She brings her own linen, flatware, china, crystal, and the centerpiece.

Centerpiece: Make a centerpiece of toys: dolls, blocks, jack-in-the-box, tops, Raggedy Ann and Andys, marbles, storybooks, trucks and cars, Tinkertoys—anything belonging to the hostess' children.

Special Feature: Hairstylist. "Hairstyles for your family" is the feature—how mothers can cut their children's hair, which shampoos are best to use, etc.

Publicity: Paint a watercolor poster of Raggedy Ann and Andy. Use cutouts from magazines also.

Theme: GRANNY'S ATTIC

Decorations: Hang quilts on the walls. Group antiques in interest centers. Drape the piano with an antique shawl.

Centerpiece: Use antiques flanked with candles for centerpieces.

Special Feature: Share the history of some unusual fashion pieces. Find some old clothes and an antique hat.

Music: Invite some grandmothers to perform songs from their era.

Program Cover: Fold patchwork wallpaper, place mats, or wrapping paper and tie with yarn.

Publicity: Use watercolors to paint a patchwork quilt with a pin cushion, needle and thread.

Encourage the ladies to wear old-fashioned clothes.

Theme: OUTER SPLENDOR

Special Feature: Fashion show. Begin the fashion show while the ladies eat. Have your own women model clothes from a local dress shop. Include wedding gowns, bridesmaid dresses, teenage clothes, and casual and formal wear.

Film: *Changepoints*—Joyce Landorf film

Discuss film in small groups. Place three suggestions on each table for discussion.

1. Share where you are right now in your own particular change-point.
2. What one thing impressed you most in the film?
3. Share a prayer need. Have conversational prayer.

Theme: SECRET PALS BIRTHDAY CELEBRATION

Refreshments: Dessert only (birthday cake)

Preparation: (Set up 12 tables, each one designating a month of the year.)

Secret Pal Revealing and Selecting:

1. *Revealing* last year's secret pal.

   Each lady brings a card for her secret pal with her own name inside, and her secret pal's name on the envelope. She places the card on the table corresponding to her secret pal's birthday month.

2. *Selecting* secret pals for coming year.

   Distribute two secret pal cards—one white for drawing, one pink duplicate "record copy" for filing. Ask interested ladies to complete both cards. The committee collects *white* filled-out cards, facedown, in a basket. Mix them up.

3. Fill out questionnaire and Family Information Sheet (all ladies). (See Appendix, pages 81-82.)

   —While answering the questionnaire, pass the basket again. All who filled out a card for secret pals will draw a card. This is your new secret pal.

   —Now, write at the top of pink cards—My secret pal is _____. Fill in the name of the person you've just drawn.

   —The committee will collect the pink cards and the questionnaires.

Get Acquainted:

1. Where were you born? (State, hospital/home)
2. What exciting or embarrassing thing has happened on one of your birthdays?
3. What was the most meaningful gift you've ever received?
4. Name a gift you'd like to bestow to someone at your table. (Example: You may say, "I give the gift of love, joy," etc.)
5. Who has most changed your life?
6. Tell us about your spiritual birthday.

Planning Details

1. Three months before the event, the director and her executive committee should choose 12 ladies (1 for each month) who will each serve as "month chairman" for her birthday month. Also, an overall event chairman should be selected.
2. The director meets with the event chairman and her month chairman to outline purpose, responsibilities, and timeline. The director has previously sent the event chairman a letter informing her and her committee of all their responsibilities. (It helps to have this in writing so there is no misunderstanding.)
3. Month chairman selects her own work team whose birthdays are in the same month as hers.

Month Chairman Responsibilities

1. Choose theme for her month.
2. Make name tags.

3. Decorate her own table. Make birthday cake for centerpiece according to the theme of her month. This should be large enough to serve all the ladies whose birthdays are in that month.
4. Bring her own paper plates, cups, and table covering.
5. Bring favors if she chooses to.
6. Make a stand-up card month for each table.
7. Clean up at the conclusion of the evening.
8. Contact and invite ladies (church ladies and visitors) with birthdays in her month. (A list of birthdays is in the office.) Give list to event chairman.
9. Recruit discussion leaders, one for every six people, whose birthdays are in her month. Give list to event chairman.

Event Chairman Responsibilities
1. Let director know how many tables are needed for each month.
2. Make sure each month chairman and her team have contacted everyone for their month. (Chairmen have a master list from office.)
3. Be the mistress of ceremonies. Be responsible for directing the discussion leaders.

Hostess tags could be placed at each table of six people. These are the discussion leaders (chosen ahead of time) and will come early to find their places. They can also help seat the ladies.

```
+----------------------------------+
|           SECRET PAL             |
| NAME _____ PHONE _____ |
| ADDRESS _____ ZIP _____ |
| BIRTHDAY _____ ANNIVERSARY ____ |
| BATH COLORS _____ |
| SCENTS _____ |
| HOBBIES _____ |
| LIKES / _____ |
+----------------------------------+
```

Suggestions
1. Send a letter to ladies who have been participants of secret pals this last year, informing them to bring a card for their secret pals for the "Revealing." Remind them to put their own name on the inside of the card and their secret pal's name on the envelope.
2. Hold two contests to be judged by the Executive Committee, with one prize for the month chairman who has chosen for her table a theme most appropriate to her month, and one prize to the month chairman who has decorated her table or cake most beautifully.
3. Choose ladies to decorate the room.
4. Draw a poster with the location of the tables in the room to display at the entrance. Hostesses will be there to help seat the ladies.
5. Have no more than six ladies sharing in a group, including the discussion leaders. Either divide the table or have round tables that only seat six.
6. Meet with director, event chairman, and discussion leader just before event for instruction, questions, purpose, and prayer.
7. Make sure you have a list of last year's secret pals at the party in case someone forgets to reveal theirs.
8. Choose someone to be responsible for secret pal files for the coming year.
9. Write a letter to all who participate in secret pals—giving them the guidelines and purpose. (See sample letter, Appendix, page 82.)
10. Give help where needed—spiritual, emotional, and physical.

RETREATS
Sample Format for One-Day Retreat

Happiness is like a butterfly—
If you chase it,
It eludes you.
If you wait patiently
It will light on your shoulder.

Theme: BE YE TRANSFORMED
Scripture: Rom. 12:26; 2 Cor. 3:18
Welcome and Introduction: 9 a.m.
Music: Theme chorus—"From Glory to Glory He's Changing Me"
Speaker:
Coffee Break: 9:45 a.m.
Workshop: 10:30 a.m.—Your choice
Workshop: 11:15 a.m.—Your choice
Lunch: 12:00 noon
Workshop: 1:15 p.m.
Meet Together: 2 p.m.—Theme chorus; speaker
Concluding Prayer: 3 p.m.

Planning Details

Centerpiece: Cut a butterfly from black construction paper. Cut out inserts for wings and glue in thin tissue paper. Place the butterflies at the base of a candle or lamp.

Favor: Butterfly magnets for refrigerator. Cut material pattern pieces and overlap together in proper place to form a butterfly. Pin together. Now stitch on sewing machine with long stitch and pull to form ruffle in center of the body. Cover center with green chenille wires. For the circled effect on the body, twist the chenille wires around a pencil and then straighten out to make the antennae. Glue magnet on the back. These favors could be used in a floral arrangement as centerpieces.

Name Tags: Make green caterpillars looking into aluminum foil mirrors. In the mirror paste a small butterfly.

Sample Format for Two-Day Retreats

Reflections of His image

Theme: REFLECTIONS OF HIS IMAGE
Scripture: 2 Cor. 3:18; Rom. 5:12
Time: Friday 6-9:30 p.m.; Saturday, 8:45 a.m.—2 p.m.
Opening Session: Friday Evening, 6 p.m.
Social Time: Table with punch and hors d'oeuvres. Hostesses circulate, greet, and introduce ladies.
Welcome and Prayer:
Dinner: Serve cafeteria style. Call tables by numbers.
Get Acquainted: Ask the lady who has a penny under her coffee cup to stand. Have everyone look at her for a moment, and then ask her to leave the room. Provide writing materials and then give the ladies the following quiz:

> Mirror, mirror on the wall—
> Who is the fair one I don't know at all?

1. What color is her hair?
2. Is it long or short? Straight or curly?
3. How tall is she?

4. What is she wearing?

5. What colors is she wearing?

6. What accessories is she wearing?

The lady returns and stands by the leader who introduces her. Review the quiz. Give prize to the winner.

Reflections on the Past: Answer on the back of a 3″ x 5″ card:

1. What was your favorite childhood toy?

2. Who had the most influence on your life?

3. Where is your favorite place to reflect or meditate?

Beginning with the hostess, go around the table and discuss. When finished, give the cards to the hostess who will turn them over to the committee. (Time: 10 minutes.)

Reflections on Special Songs: Sing favorite songs or choruses.

Reflections on the Word: Looking into God's Word and into your hearts. Introduce the Bible studies for the year. (Have study books available for purchase.)

Introduction of Speaker and Theme: "Reflecting His Image . . . Confidently"

Looking Within: Hostesses have been given two questions from the speaker's topic. Leader opens discussion on the questions and table hostesses continue it, concluding with a prayer. (Time: 10 minutes.)

Chorus: "Turn Your Eyes upon Jesus (Sung without accompaniment while some groups may still be praying.)

Saturday Morning, 8:45 a.m.

Devotions (based on Ps. 17:15, NIV—David's Prayer)

Breakfast

Break (15 minutes)

Choruses (as ladies return)

Speaker: "Walking in His Image—Joyfully"

Small-Group Discussion: Hostesses stand and all ladies with the same color name tag as hostess will go with her to another room for small-group discussion. The hostess will give each lady the following sheet for group interaction. (Time: 30 minutes.)

Read 2 Cor. 3:1-18 and discuss the following questions:

1. When was a time that Christ helped you particularly to be confident and competent? (verses 5-6, NIV).

2. In which of your relationships do you feel you most reflect the "radiance of his glory"? (verses 17-18, NIV).

3. What verse in this passage impressed you most? How can you apply it to your life?

4. What can you do to reflect God's glory in ever-increasing measure? (James 1:22-25).

Snack Break

Speaker: "His Image for Me—Becoming"

Open Sharing: General sharing of personal reflections on: "What the retreat meant to me" or "What Christ is doing in my life."

Announcement: Attention is called to the evaluation sheets that were placed on the tables before the session. All are urged to fill them out and give them to the hostesses before leaving.

Closing: Form a circle, hold hands, and sing "We Are One in the Bond of Love."

Conclusion: Place a small bouquet of straw flowers (each individual bouquet with flowers all of the same color) at each setting before the morning meeting. Each lady takes her bouquet and exchanges individual straw flowers with other ladies, sharing reflections of love and appreciation. Everyone thus takes home a many-colored bouquet—"Reflections of Love."

Planning Details for the Retreat

Meals: Preferably catered. (Chairman will have already discussed menus and prices and selected caterer.)

Colors: White tablecloths, orange/brown napkins, brown candles

Snacks:
1. On Saturday ladies bring one cup of fresh fruit for fruit bowl.
2. Committee makes coffee cake.
3. Hostesses bring cheese and crackers.

Centerpiece—Materials Needed:

Two 5″ x 7″ mirrors

Tape, blue

Two pictures of Christ

9″ x 9″ square (or round) mirror

Spray of dried flowers

The two mirrors are taped together on the back so that they hinge at the top to form an easel. Stand the easel on the round or square mirror.

Scrape an area off the back of the standing mirrors and place the picture of Christ in the opening so that the picture is surrounded by the remaining mirror. Arrange the spray of dried flowers on the mirror base. (Sometime during the retreat sell the centerpieces at cost.)

Favor: Small mirror with picture of Christ inserted as in table decoration. A magnet could be put on the back and used on refrigerator.

Program Cover:

Construction paper in fall colors

Aluminum foil (or small round mirrors)

Gold braid—to go around mirror

Gold cording for the cover fold

Name Tags and Hostess Tags:

Construction paper—eight different colors cut in shape of hand mirror

Circular white paper (for mirror part)

Ribbon—fall colors

Make one hostess tag of each color to match small groups. Make smaller "mirrors" for regular name tags in colors corresponding to those of hostesses. Eventually groups will be formed of those with the same color.

Variations on Ladies' Retreats

Theme: MAKE LOVE YOUR AIM
Scripture: Col. 3:14

Name Tags: Big red hearts (Suggest that each lady wear red, white, or pink.)

Decorations: Valentine arrangements

Favors: Red satin hearts with lace

Sharing Time: Cut a puzzle from a large roll of white butcher paper. Give everyone a big piece of the puzzle. Ask each lady to draw on her puzzle piece in picture, word, or symbol, the place in her home that she considers the "warmest" or her "favorite" place. Also, illustrate the "coolest" or her "least favorite" place. In turn, place the puzzle pieces on the floor, and ask each lady to explain her drawing.

Game: Each table makes a valentine for another table.

Music: Old love songs (printed in program)

And over all these virtues put on love, which binds them all together in perfect unity.

Col. 3:14, NIV

Theme: DOORWAYS AND DISCOVERIES

Scripture: 2 Cor. 2:12

Get Acquainted: Discoveries . . . Getting to Know You

At each place a card is placed with the list of weather conditions given below. Each lady is to mark the one that most closely describes her feelings at that moment.

    a. sunny and warm

    b. overcast

c. stormy

d. rainy, but expected to clear

e. cold and wintry

f. hot and humid

g. not a cloud in the sky

h. tepid

i. a howling blizzard

j. scattered showers

k. clear, brisk, invigorating

l. a tornado watch

Special Feature—Opening Doors:

Present a booklet containing the plans and special events for the upcoming year. (See Appendix, 76.) This is an ideal time to get women involved in Bible studies, prayer groups, and other ministries.

Speaker: Topic—"Discoveries"

At the conclusion of the message, form into groups according to name tag colors for discussion. After 10 minutes have one person from each group report to the whole group her group's "discoveries."

Saturday Morning

Breakfast: A Scripture Promise bookmark is put at each place. Use "promise box" cards. Punch a hole in the upper left corner and tie a colorful bow. This can be a personal promise for the entire year. At each table, have the promises read aloud, with each lady sharing thoughts on how to apply this to life right now. Conclude with prayer.

Speaker:

Planning Details

Centerpiece: Except for the head table, fall flower arrangements can be brought in by hostesses. The centerpiece for the head table may consist of a simulated door made from Styrofoam (6½″ x 12″). An oval window is cut out and colored cellophane inserted. Wood-grain Con-Tact paper is pasted over the Styrofoam door. A small metal bell may be glued on for a doorknob. Fasten the door to the Styrofoam base with toothpicks. Place small vases of straw flowers on porch. Cut "WELCOME" from black construction paper and pin to base.

Program Covers: Make a construction paper door with a cutout window to show theme underneath.

Name Tags: Use actual leaves pasted on cards or cut out from fall-colored construction paper.

Theme: WALK WORTHY

Scripture: Col. 1:10

Get Acquainted: Place 3″ x 5″ cards at each setting and have the women write answers to the following:

1. What is your name, room number, address, church?
2. What was the best thing that happened to you today?
3. What pair of shoes have you owned that hurt your feet but you wore them anyway? When and why?

Share answers for about 10 minutes.

Evening Devotions: In each room place suggestions for bedtime devotions, which are to be shared with roommates.

Guidelines as follows:

Read 1 John 1:7—"If we walk in the light, as he is in the light, we have fellowship with one another, and the blood of Jesus, his Son, purifies us from all sin" (NIV).

1. Share a time in your life when you were walking in the shadow.
2. Share a time when you were walking in the sunlight.
3. How can you walk worthy as a saleslady for Jesus Christ?
4. Do you have any dark spots in your life at the present time?
5. Pray for one another.

Saturday Morning Devotions: (During that second cup of coffee— around the breakfast tables) Give these discussion questions to the hostesses earlier.

Read Col. 1:10.

1. How can I know that I am walking worthily and pleasing God in my life? Discuss.
2. As I walk into my day today, for what can I thank God?
3. Do I have a need that I would like to share?

Have conversational prayer.

Song: "The Greatest Thing in All My Life Is Loving You"
(Verse 2: "Knowing You"; Verse 3: "Serving You")

Fun Questions: After breakfast write the following information on the cards at your place.

1. Name, address, church, room number
2. What funny thing happened last night?
3. What new thing did you find out about your roommate?
4. Who is sitting on your right? What is her hobby?

Share responses. Collect. (At various times during the day read some of the responses aloud to the entire group.)

Small Groups: Divide into groups of 10 and discuss these questions:

1. Whose shoes would you like to walk in for a day? Why?
2. What was the most memorable walk you've ever taken? Why?
3. Where are you in your walk with Christ right now?

Have conversational prayer.

Planning Details

Centerpiece: Make a ceramic old-fashioned shoe and paint it brown and ivory. Fill this with fresh yellow and white daisies, greenery, baby's breath. Tie a yellow checked gingham bow to the top of the shoe. (Each finished centerpiece costs about $3.75 to make.) One of the Sunday School classes may take this on as a special project. A hobby shop owner can teach you how to make the shoe step by step—cleaning, firing, glazing, firing, painting, spraying. Sell them at the retreat for $10.00.

Individual Favors: A Barbie doll boot can be painted ivory (only florist paint will adhere to plastic) and filled with assorted colored straw flowers. First, however, fill with rock salt to stabilize. Wire a tiny yellow gingham bow to the top of the boot. Stuff with cotton.

Program Covers: Cut brown Holly Hobbie girls out of gift wrapping paper and glue onto buff-colored construction paper.

Name Tags and Hostess Tags: Cut name tags in the form of a shoe from 10 colors of construction paper (or use as many colors as needed, depending upon the number of small groups you desire).

Theme: WOMEN FASHIONED BY GOD

Scripture: Col. 3:14 (TLB)

Sharing Time: During dessert, have each one around the table respond to these two questions:

1. What was the best thing that happened to you today?
2. What were you doing at 2 p.m. today? Describe your situation.

Small Groups: Discuss these questions:

1. What woman do you most admire? What qualities of beauty does she possess? How has she influenced your life?
2. How is God fashioning you into a more beautiful woman?

Saturday Morning Devotions: (with your roommates)

1. Look up these scriptures and share how they can help you become a more beautiful person.
   a. Body—Rom. 12:1
   b. Mind—Rom. 12:2; Isa. 26:3
   c. Spirit (behavior)—1 Pet. 3:3-5
2. What discipline do you need to develop?

Pray together

Small Groups: Hostesses should distribute seven self-adhesive address labels to each lady in her group. Starting with the one on the hostess's right, each lady becomes the center of a "Ceremony of Affirmation."

Every other lady writes on an address label a brief, signed, complimentary note to the one in the "center." One by one, beginning with the hostess, they read what they have written and then hand it to the person. She sticks them on the inside back cover of her notebook. Then they go on to the next lady, who becomes the center of this affirming attention. This continues all the way around the circle until the leader (last) is also affirmed. When finished, each woman will have seven (assuming there are eight persons at the table) complimentary reflections in her notebook.

Centerpiece: Cameo plaque arrangement. Colors—blue, gold, and white.

Purchase a cameo mold (6½″ x 4½″) at a hobby shop. Stick a hairpin in the back of the cameo while plaster of paris is still damp so the plaque can be hung later.

Paint a blue background, white cameo, and gold frame; also, a black cameo with a white background makes a beautiful contrast.

Place the cameo plaque on a frame stand. Center this on a 9″ x 9″ mirror. A long-stem blue carnation with a gold ribbon bow on the stem is laid across the mirror. The scripture is attached to the streamer of the bow.

For favors, cameo candy can be bought; however, at the hobby shop you can buy cameo candy molds, white chocolate, colored food paste, and the recipe. This is much cheaper and fun to do. The *Ideals* candy booklet sold at the hobby shop gives directions for using two colors also.

Another idea for a favor is a cameo magnet for the refrigerator. Use a candy mold (other than the one in which you made candy) for small plaster of paris cameos. Press two magnets on the back while the plaster of paris is still damp. Or put in a hairpin during molding to create a small hanging cameo. Paint the background blue (or any other color you may choose) and the cameo white.

Name Tags and Programs: For name tags, draw a cameo on gold construction paper. Make the programs of sturdy gold paper with same design as the name tag. Fill in with black Magic Marker.

Theme: LIVING TO SERVE
Scripture: Josh. 24:15

Program Cover: Cover sturdy-weight paper with wallpaper to make a house. In the door of the house write the theme verse. In the window appears the motto—"Living to Serve." Use houses throughout all your planning.

Welcomer: Give a *potholder* to each lady with her motel key (if applicable) and a little welcome message pinned to the potholder.

Centerpieces: Make tea cozies shaped like houses. Put a little votive candle by each one. Sometime during the retreat have a silent auction for the centerpieces, asking the ladies to write their bids on slips of paper. Top bidders get first chance to buy.

Wall Decoration: Cut a large house out of plain heavy paper. Glue its roof with the matching wallpaper used on the programs. Write out Josh. 24:15 in the window and the theme (Living to Serve) in large letters on the side of the house.

Favors: Give a favor at each meal.

1. Give a clothespin (long type) with theme printed on it and tied with matching bow. Tuck a dust cloth in the clothespin to remind the ladies of serving at home. This material could match the window curtains on the programs and on the wall decorations.
2. A "mock" doormat in blue loose-woven material that is fringed on all sides is a good place card.
3. A dough-art plaque on which the theme verse is spelled out with alphabet soup letters glued and painted.

Name Tags: Make houses from construction paper.

Share: Have each partner share (1) one room in your heart that God has been working on, cleaning out, or remodeling; (2) a new room you know He wants to begin working on.

Theme: HATS OFF TO YOU

Get Acquainted: Every lady must wear a hat to get into Friday night's dinner. During dinner, one from each table tells the story of her hat.

Game: Give each table a bag with a roll of bathroom tissue, tape, pins, and a large hat. Ask the ladies to decorate the hat with the bathroom tissue and items from their purses. Model the hat and name it.

Name Tags: Make construction-paper hats. Pin with hat pins.

Decorations: Straw hats, upside down, with flowers inside.

Favors: Turn Styrofoam cups upside down and bake them in an oven. They become hats. Decorate them with ribbon and flowers.

Theme: GROWING IN CHRIST

Scripture: Eph. 3:17

Centerpieces: Wicker watering pots with silk and dried flower arrangements. (Sell these during retreat.)

Favors: (one at each meal)

1. Vase made out of a wooden bead with straw flowers inserted. Small round circle with theme "Growing in Christ" is tied to stems of straw flowers.
2. Round magnetic refrigerator cork with theme and a flower.
3. Small bouquet of dried flowers in bundle. Have five or six colors of flowers, but make each bundle only one color. To close, have the ladies exchange flowers from their bouquet with others.

Name Tags: Silk flower with name on leaf. Use eight different colors for eight small groups.

Program: On title page glue a mustard seed to a small plant drawing—each consecutive page shows plant growing.

Door Prizes: Three or four small plastic watering pots filled with potpourri. Award these to the lady with the most trees in her yard, the lady with the oldest tree, and similar descriptions.

Welcomer: Place small potted plants and a welcome sheet in the rooms for each lady before check-in time of the retreat. Example: Welcome to "Growing in Christ" Ladies' Retreat. We hope you will relax and enjoy yourself. We have been praying for you—by name—and trust God will work in your life this weekend to help "your roots to grow down deep into the soil of God's marvelous love." See you at 6 p.m. in the banquet room!

Room Devotions—Bedtime Devotions, Friday Evening:

1. Read Eph. 3:17-19 (TLB)
2. Read Eph. 3:17-19 (KJV)
3. Read Eph. 3:17-19 (Phillips)
4. Read Eph. 3:17-19 (NEB)

Share something you particularly liked in these verses.

Room Devotions—Saturday Morning:

1. Read Ps. 35:28 and Ps. 51:15.
2. Jesus prays constantly for us—that makes us prayer partners with Him! Spend some time in conversational prayer with your roommate praising and thanking our Heavenly Father. Read Ps. 51:15 again.
3. Include a time of seeking His guidance and blessing for today.
4. As we begin this new day, let's see if, as the Psalmist says, His praise can be on our tongue *and* in our hearts all the day long. "Praise, like sunlight, helps all things grow." Read Ps. 35:28 again.

Small Group—Friday Night:

1. Tell your first, middle, and last name, and your favorite flower.
2. Describe your favorite way of spending spare time. What does it do for you?
3. What character qualities draw you to another person? (honesty, patience, gentleness, etc.)
4. When was the first time God became more than a name to you?
5. What has God done for you today?
6. How has God helped you grow recently?

Small Group—Saturday Morning:

1. What is something you have enjoyed watching grow?
2. What are some similar characteristics between a plant growing and a Christian growing?

    —John 12:24-25, *depth*   —Eph. 3:17, *roots grow deeper*
    —Ps. 1:3, *fruitbearing*   —Col. 2:7
    —Ps. 92:13, *growth*   —John 15:2, *needs pruning*
    —1 Pet. 2:2   —John 15:5, *sap flowing from*
    —2 Pet. 3:18   *vine to all parts*
    of the plant

3. What are the necessary ingredients for plant growth? Compare these to spiritual growth.

    —Matt. 13:23, *Seed*   *God's Word*
    —John 8:12, *Light*   *Jesus, the Light*
    —John 3:18, *Sun*   *God's Son*
    —Col. 1:13
    —Matt. 14:33
    —Eph. 3:17, *Soil*   *Soil of God's love* (grace)
    —John 4:34, *Food*   *Our meat/food is doing God's will*
    —Ps. 1:3, *Water*   *Living Water*

Small Group—Saturday Afternoon:

1. Memorize Eph. 3:17. *(a)* Pass out memory cards. Have each person write the verse as you read. *(b)* Call on someone to read entire selection off of their card. *(c)* Have each person read the same first phrase. *(d)* Go around circle, each person saying one word at a time. Complete this and repeat it two times, beginning with a different person each time. *(e)* Have each person say the phrase from memory. *(f)* When completed, repeat each phrase from memory; then the whole verse.
2. Share one area of growth God has helped you with recently, or

one area in which you need to grow.

3. As time allows tell what has been most helpful or meaningful to you in this retreat.

SEASONAL ACTIVITIES

VALENTINE'S DAY

Special Features:

1. Ask a few husbands in advance to write something unusual, funny, or special about their wives and send to the mistress of ceremonies. Read aloud during the program.
2. Show slides of couples' weddings or early years together.
3. Have your church photographer take pictures of couples at the banquet at a reduced price. Prepare a special background for this.
4. Interview a couple about their first impressions of one another. Ask about their first date, proposal, wedding, honeymoon, etc.
5. Skit—"Ribs, Fig Leaves, and Apples" (see page 55).

Centerpieces:

1. Use red and white carnations with lots of greenery. Glue paper hearts on chenille wires and put into arrangement.
2. Paint a tree branch white. Hang red hearts from the branch to make a mobile.
3. Cut two wooden hearts of different sizes with a hole drilled in the top. Sand; paint red. Put white candle in each heart and place on mirrors. Place a long-stem rose or carnation with a red ribbon bow across the mirror.
4. Use round 8-inch diameter Styrofoam to make base. Glue red ribbon around the edge and a doily on the top. Straighten out a coat hanger and cover with red tape. Stick this through a 3″ wide red net, and gather enough to make a ruffle. Shape the hanger at the top to form a heart and stick the ends down into opposite edges of base. Place a white plastic cupid (hollow inside) on a dowel stick that has been stuck into center of base. Surround this with red silk roses and baby's breath.

MOTHER'S DAY
Mother/Daughter Events

Special Features:

1. Select a panel of five mother/daughter teams. Seat them in chairs back-to-back, mothers opposite their daughters. As the moderator asks questions, the contestants write their answers on a 9″ x 9″ card and hold it up for everyone to see. If

mother/daughter sets match perfectly, they receive a point. Both mothers and daughters write answers to the following questions.

To Daughters:
1. Where was your mother born?
2. When did your father propose to your mother?
3. What is your mom's favorite color?

To Mothers:
4. Who was your daughter's favorite teacher?
5. Who was your daughter's first boyfriend?
6. What is your daughter's favorite food?

To Daughters: (bonus question)
7. What is your dad's nickname for your mother?

2. Any lady interested can model her own wedding dress, her mother's, or someone else's. A narrator tells about each dress, and a story or incident that goes with it. Play wedding music throughout the fashion show.

3. Appoint a committee weeks before the banquet. They select the mother they feel has made or is making the most outstanding contributions in her home, church, and community. She is crowned at the banquet by the reigning Mother of the Year. Her name is engraved on a plaque, and she is presented with an arm bouquet of flowers.

Centerpieces:

1. Theme: Rising to New Heights. Attach helium-filled balloons to flowerpots filled with assorted flowers. Balloons are multicolored.
2. Theme: King's Daughter. Make crowns out of gold-foil covered cardboard and decorate with jewels. Arrange fresh flowers in the center of crown.

Mother/Daughter Banquet

Theme: PATTERN FOR LIVING

Program: Make a pattern envelope. Place the illustrated sheets in the envelope.

Front of envelope   Back of envelope

For directions on how to make the envelope and contents, see Appendix, pages 83-87.

Game: Take sheet four out of the envelope. Give to each lady a small envelope containing little pieces of material representing the answers.

Get Acquainted: Pass a spool of thread at each table and ask the ladies to cut off a piece. Have them twist the thread around their fingers, telling about themselves until the thread is finished.

CHRISTMAS

Special Features:

1. Christmas is a good time to honor longtime members by asking the following questions:
   —Who has been a member the greatest number of years?
   —Who was the first lady here to get married in this church?
   —Who grew up in this church and married a boy from here also?
   —Who joined the church between the years 1920-30? 1930-40? As time permits, continue other decades. (Have winners come to the microphone to be interviewed and receive a prize.)

   Interview questions:
   —What brought you to this church?
   —Who was your pastor?
   —What was happening in your life at that time?

2. Ask every person attending to bring a Christmas card. (Have extras available for those who forget.) Place small white slips of paper at each table and conduct the exchange in the following sequence:
   —Ask everyone to write his or her name on a slip of paper and fold it.
   —Put the ladies' names in a white sack with a red bow.
   —Put the men's names in a brown sack with a green bow.
   —Pass the sacks again and have each person draw out a name— men draw men's names and ladies draw ladies' names.
   —Select a Santa Claus. (Ask three men to audition their "Ho Ho Ho's." Respond by applause. The winner is Santa Claus for the evening.)
   —Ask everyone to write two things on the Christmas card to the person whose name he or she has drawn. (1) Something you appreciate about them; (2) Something you would like to do for them.
   —Have Santa Claus collect all the cards in a basket and redistribute to the person whose name is on the envelope.
   —One at a time, read the cards aloud around your tables.

Sharing:

1. The following are some questions that can stimulate sharing around the table:
   —What toy was your favorite Christmas present?
   —What was your most unusual Christmas ever? Why?
   —Where did you spend Christmas when you were 12 years old?
   —What Christmas traditions do you observe? What was your very best Christmas, or the one you remember the most? Why?
   —Who or what from the Nativity scene is your favorite figure? Why?
   —What gift would you like to give to the whole world?
   —What was the most treasured gift you ever received?

2. Before the meeting ask five ladies to be prepared to tell the

group about a treasured gift they have received. If possible, have them bring the gift to show.

3. Place Christmas cards beside each plate. Have the ladies write inside the cards something they would like to do for another lady present. Collect the cards and redistribute randomly. Provide time later for getting together and making plans to do whatever.

4. Use a fruit and candy basket for the centerpiece. Under it put the name, address, and some information about a needy family or shut-in from your church. (You could collect an offering to pay for the baskets.) Choose someone from your table to deliver the basket and pray together for this family.

Centerpieces:

1. Assign ladies to bring a Christmas candle decoration. On either side of the candle, place red and green wrapped gift packages, interspersed with Christmas tree ornaments.

2. Have your committee or a Sunday School class bring fruit, nuts, cookies, and foil-wrapped homemade candy. Collect baskets of different sizes. Wrap the fruit baskets in clear paper, tie with a big bow, and add lots of color.

Favors:

Wrap small boxes of matches in the same red or green design Christmas paper, alternating the colors at the place settings. Punch a hole in the end of the box. Tie with yarn and a tag with the message "As you light your Christmas candles, remember the Light of the World."

Name Tags:

1. Mimeograph a white or red bell. Glue on green leaves and red berries.

2. Stick-on Christmas tags

Christmas Craft Ideas:

1. Hold a boutique in two homes near one another. The ladies of the church may help decorate several rooms in each. Bring hand-made craft items and homemade baked goodies. Serve refreshments at each home, and give door prizes.

2. Decorate several homes early for Christmas. Select themes for each home. Sell craft items in each home that follow its particular theme. Some ideas:
   —Baked items—gingerbread house, gingerbread men, Christmas desserts, breads, cookies, and suckers (homemade) wrapped with plastic wrap and tied with ribbons
   —Crocheted, knitted, or sewn items
   —Dough art—tree decorations, wreaths, centerpieces
   —Wood items
   —Ceramics
   Each hostess can enlist other ladies to help her make crafts and decorate her home.

3. To beat the Christmas rush, schedule a silent auction near the second week in November. Limit all entries to "homemade" items. On the designated day put a 3″ x 5″ card by each item with the name of the item and a minimum bid written at the top. This minimum bid is what the materials for the item cost or a reasonable sale price suggested by the one who made it. Invite people to come and browse and then serve lunch. After lunch, ladies can look and write bids on the 3″ x 5″ cards. (Give people ample time to look again at their selections in case someone outbid them.) When the emcee calls time, bidding ceases and the last name on the 3″ x 5″ card gets to buy her selection.

3

Program Features

GET-ACQUAINTED GAMES

Creative Hands
Four Happy Events
Getting to Know You
Pleasant Experience
All About Me
Sing Together
Descriptive Name Tags
Associations
Footsteps to Friendship
Let Love Guide Your Life
Friendship Calendar
Find Someone Who Can Say . . .

SKITS, READINGS, DEVOTIONALS

A Fun Fashion Skit
Katie Krazy Style Show
Ribs, Fig Leaves, and Apples
The Reigning Queen
"Mother"

The Ideal Mother
A Little Parable for Mother
To His Mother
What Is a Daughter?
Proverbs 31:10-31: A Paraphrase
The Padded Cross
I Said a Prayer for You Today
If Jesus Came to Your House
Someone Had Prayed
The Housewife
The Teacher
Jis' Blue
Test Prayer
A Prayer for Parents
An Evening Prayer

COMMUNION SERVICES

Traditional
Agape Love Feast
One-on-One

3 Program Features

Creative program features will make your special event more fun for everyone. Here is a potpourri of ideas—games, poems, skits, and devotionals —to make a good event better.

GET-ACQUAINTED GAMES

Creative Hands

As they arrive, give each lady a colored sheet of construction paper with a straight pin in it. (Use one color per group—between six and eight to a group.) Instruct each one to tear the paper into a design that represents an interest, hobby, or vocation, and to pin it on her dress. (These can double as name tags.) Have the women form a circle with those whose tags are the same color. Each one introduces herself and everyone guesses what her design represents.

Four Happy Events

On 3″ x 5″ cards have each person draw a straight line to represent her life. Then, on that line, mark four dots that represent four happy events in her life. In small groups share what those events were.

Getting to Know You

Get acquainted by asking one or two others the following questions:
1. What is your hometown?
2. What was your favorite childhood pet, and why did you love it?
3. What is the happiest vacation you have ever taken?
4. What would you like to do if you had a day off?

Pleasant Experience

Give each lady a 3″ x 5″ card. Ask her to write on the card a pleasant experience she has had recently. Scramble the cards in a box, and ask each lady to draw one and find the person who wrote about the experience.

All About Me

Get acquainted by asking one or two others the following questions:
1. What is your favorite TV program? Why?
2. What would be your dream vacation?
3. What was the happiest day of your life?
4. If you were to get a telegram in the mail when you get home tonight, what would it say?

Sing Together

As the ladies arrive, give each the name of a familiar song. (The same song title should be given to six or eight people.) Ring a bell as a signal for everyone to begin singing their songs and forming a group by locating those who are singing the same song. Designate as leader that person whose name begins with the letter closest to *A*. Beginning with the leader, each should introduce herself and answer the following questions:

1. Are you married or single?
2. What was the funniest thing that happened to you this week?
3. What one thing happened that turned your thoughts to God?
4. What are you happy about today?

Descriptive Name Tags

Construction paper should be given to each woman as she arrives to make a name tag. Under her name, she is to write five words ending in the letters "ing" to describe herself. These can be shared in groups of three or four.

Associations

Give each lady a card with a word written on it. Give another lady the opposite of that word. Have opposites find one another and share three things about themselves.

Other get-acquainted games are pictured on the succeeding pages:

Footsteps to Friendship
Let Love Guide Your Life
Friendship Calendar
Find Someone Who Can Say . . .

Footsteps to Friendship

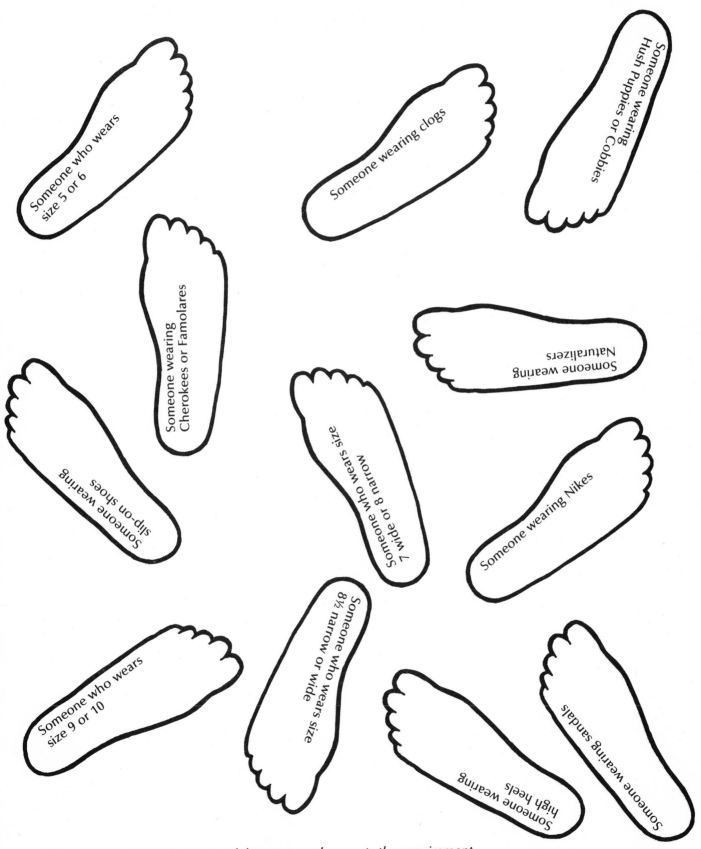

Someone who wears size 5 or 6

Someone wearing clogs

Someone wearing Hush Puppies or Cobbies

Someone wearing Cherokees or Famolares

Someone wearing Naturalizers

Someone wearing slip-on shoes

Someone who wears size 7 wide or 8 narrow

Someone wearing Nikes

Someone who wears size 9 or 10

Someone who wears size 8½ narrow or wide

Someone wearing high heels

Someone wearing sandals

Write in the footprint the name of the person who meets the requirement.

49

Let Love Guide Your Life

Please get the *signature* of a person who meets the following requirements:

1. Someone who was born in the same month you were. _____

2. Someone who was born in the same state you were. _____

3. Someone who has the same color eyes you have. _____

4. Someone whose first name you did not know. _____

5. Someone who has lived outside the continental U.S.A. _____

6. Someone who had a baby within this last year. _____

7. Someone who has been married less than five years. _____

8. Someone who is an elementary schoolteacher. _____

9. Someone who has attended this church for more than 10 years. _____

10. Someone who has joined this church in the last year. _____

11. Someone who is wearing a dress the same color you are. _____

12. Someone who has the same number of letters in her first name. _____

13. Someone who has three or more grandchildren. _____

14. Find two people who have the same first name. _____

    _____

15. Find two people who are relatives. _____

    _____

16. Someone who plays a musical instrument other than the piano or organ. _____

    _____

Friendship Calendar

Name _____

January	February	March	April
May	June	July	August
September	October	November	December

Distribute the Friendship Calendar to each lady. Find ladies to sign their birthday month.

Find Someone Who Can Say . . .

I'm left-handed.	I have been to the dentist this month.	We were born in the same month.	My husband is bald.	I have a child less than one year old.	I can knit or do needlework.
I collect something alive for a hobby.	I have six or more brothers and sisters.	I've had my appendix out.	I was born in California.	My husband wears glasses.	We are the same height.
We wear the same size shoe.	We were born in the same year.	I play more than one musical instrument.	I can slalom ski.	My husband is a sports nut.	I sing alto in the church choir.
I LOVE LIVER.	Sign your own name.	I have green eyes.	I like rare meat.	I've lived in _____ (your city) more than five years.	I jog three times a week.
I've been married less than five years.	My favorite color is blue.	I own a Volkswagen.	I have a child older than 21.	I love to go camping.	I wear contacts.
I have red hair.	My favorite color is yellow.	I love horseback riding.	I LOVE chocolate.	My middle name is Anne.	I play softball.

SKITS • READINGS DEVOTIONALS

A Fun Fashion Skit
by Marie Gilbert

ANNOUNCER: The fashions you will see are exclusive. You may be sure you will never see them duplicated anywhere at any price.

1. "Our first model has selected a duster for early morning wear. It is of waffle piqué with the ever-popular Peter Pan collar. Notice the attractive copper buttons. Her feet are snugly encased in honey bun slippers." (Costume is a short housecoat with waffles pinned on it, with copper scouring pads for buttons. Collar is made of foil pie pans. Old sandals or slippers have sweet buns attached.)

2. "The next model is wearing a daytime dress featuring the latest in cap sleeves and a smart pencil slim skirt. To complete the ensemble she has chosen a fashionable sailor hat, the popular string gloves, and a smart but serviceable bucket bag." (Bottle caps or baseball caps are fastened on the upper sleeves of an old blouse. Pencils are cellophane-taped all over the slim skirt. Hat is old white duck sailor hat with brim turned down. White gloves have strings hanging from the fingertips. Bag is a bucket with a ribbon tied on the handle.)

3. "Our next model wears the ever-chic nylon box jacket suit in the season's most popular color, cedar brown. Note the bone buttons and the extreme but fetching earrings to match. The suit skirt is of basket weave and the hat is a 'Jackie' pillbox model. Note the ultimate in the envelope handbag." (Jacket is a large cardboard box covered with old nylon stockings. The bone buttons and earrings are dog biscuits. Fasten small size berry baskets to strings of various lengths to cover the skirt. Pillboxes are arranged on any old hat. The purse is a large manila envelope.)

4. "Now we have the belle of the beach, who is wearing the latest in bathing apparel—a coverall bathing suit for complete sunburn protection. It concentrates its sparkling appeal on neck, wrist, ankle, and back interest. Multicolored straw hat and bag complete the ensemble." (Bathing suit is man's coverall or long underwear with abundant junk jewelry at the neck, wrist, and ankles, and on the back flap. Colored soda straws decorate the hat and bag.)

5. "Now if you are looking for a late afternoon tea dress you will be interested in the next model. Her frock is made of the finest tissue, with an attractive scoop neckline. She has chosen a rolled hat to match her dress. Dainty T-strap pumps flatter her feet." (Plain straight dress is covered with cleansing tissues, tasseled with tea bags. Plastic scoop is worn around the neck, and tea bags are tied to the shoes. A roll of tissue tied with a ribbon is her hat.)

6. "Evening elegance is personified in our next model, who wears a 14-carat gold gown with a plunging neckline. Clever accessories include a hold-everything mesh bag and dainty mitts. The chapeau is the newest spring model for after five." (Plain dress dyed gold with 14 carrots trimming it. A small rubber plunger is worn around the neck. The bag is an old mesh bag used for oranges or onions. It contains everything including a toy kitchen sink. Baseball mitts are worn and springs decorate the hat.)

7. "Last, but not least, comes a model for evening wear at home. Its flowing lines make for complete relaxation." (A full, long-sleeved, old-fashioned nightshirt and nightcap. Model carries an alarm clock and hot water bottle.) —Used by permission from *Kitchen Klatter* magazine, May 1966.

Katie's Krazy Style Show

Announcer: *Commentary on Style Show*

"No matter what the season—winter, summer, spring, or fall—all of us are naturally interested in what's new in the world of fashion. To help you select your new wardrobe, we've assembled a few of the really significant models, the cream of the couturier's crop. We have apparel for morning, afternoon, and evening. These we are now pleased to present."

1. "Our first style is the one I'm wearing. One never knows, does one, when one may be called upon to be a Toastmistress? How handy, then, to have this little frock, just made for the occasion! Ladies and gents— the Toastmistress! There's a certain feeling of crispness here from bosom to thigh. This is really hot stuff in all the large Paris salons. The sombre shade is Dior's burnt bread. This is one of those you can dress up or down. To add a little sparkle, try lacing it with a little honey, peanut butter, or a spot of raspberry jam." (Toast about three loaves of bread, fasten on a plain dress. Make necklace of chunks of toast. Hat—loaf of rye bread. Bag—an old toaster.)

2. "Next, that important little suit, the sort of thing you can actually live in—it goes anywhere. We proudly present the newest of the silhouettes, 'The Box Suit.' Note the simple, clean-cut lines and also how the shoes carry out the feel of the suit. The purse too is right—by Kellogg's. In choosing this we were aware of its great adaptability. It's useful when you're not wearing it, as a storage place for Junior's tricycle or that lovely lampshade Grandma made." (A large box from the grocery store [at least 36 inches deep]. Cut a hole in top and slip over the head. Paint or cover with wallpaper. Hat box for the hat, shoe box for shoes, box of Kellogg's breakfast food for purse.)

3. "Now for the all-important little afternoon frock—the print. This is an up-to-the-minute, right-off-the-press number. It might be said to have all the print that's fit for news, if I may coin a phrase. To get the undivided attention of the man in your life, just wear the sports edition where it can be easily read from his seat on the bus. This little number is also right for breakfast wear. At least hubby will be looking at *you* instead of holding the morning edition on the table." (Newspaper for dress. Fold two pieces of newspaper for hat and purse.)

4. "This year, as always, cotton ranks high. You might even say the ranker, the higher, so we used considerable care in our selection. Here, as before, we had an eye to the all-round usefulness of this dress—the little cool cotton. Notice the unusual treatment of the cotton. The earrings are by Q-tips, the hat is an original by Mountain Mist, and the purse is by Johnson and Johnson. One of the nice things about this little outfit is that you're ready for anything from Sonny's nosebleed to sopping up baby's ice cream cone." (Use a plain dress with cotton puffs or cotton batting sewed on it. Use any hat covered with cotton. Purse—a package of cotton with cord handle. Fix earrings with two Q-tips tied together and hung over ears.)

5. "Comes now the dream dress! Who has not longed to see herself in lace? I'm happy to say this little creation in exquisite lace is no longer prohibitive in price. Neckline news is high in fashion. In front, the doily look, and in back—the plunging neckline. Her hat is an original by Royale and the jewelry is by Mad Moments." (Use plain dress. Fasten doilies together and let them hang around the waist like a tunic. Trim collar with doilies. Tie a sink plunger around the neck, letting it hang down the back. Large round doily for hat. Lots of gaudy jewelry.)

6. "For those who like a touch of elegance in fabric and line, we have the Drape Dress. Note how cleverly the material is handled as no one but Kirsch knows how to do it. It's just a bit daring; in fact, you might call it slightly risqué. I'd say it's all of that. Try running to the phone in this and see what happens. You risk your neck at every leap. Confidentially, may I say that it's perfect for you who are trying to conceal 'the battle of the bulge' or for those who are infanticipating." (Use drapery rods across shoulder with drapes on rings, hanging full in front and trailing behind. Flowered drapes best.)

7. "For the woman who may or may not be watching her weight, there is the dinner gown by Eatmore and Bulge. This one is an absolute must. Note the lovely turtleneck—no, it's a chicken neck. Should your date stand you up, you'll be equal to the occasion with this vitamin-packed creation." (Sew paper dinner plates all over plain dress. Glue pictures of food in center of plates. Cover fried chicken with plastic wrap and tie around the neck for a necklace. Secure coffee pot on paper plate and tie under chin for a hat.)

8. "With afternoon teas becoming increasingly popular, the tea gown grows more important. This one is a copy of a design by Sir Thomas Lipton. It's serviceable. The English are so-o-o practical! It saves dashing back and forth to the kitchen as the guests arrive. One simply tears off another bag, dunks, and serves. The chapeau by Cannon is simply mopping clean across the land." (Tea bags sewn all over plain dress. Lemon slices for earrings, or plastic cups from a child's tea set. Necklace of sugar cubes. Hat—a kitchen towel.)

9. "For you younger girls we have something really special. It's called the 'Date Dress.' A great help for those who are inclined to forget engagements. Our former model died mysteriously while watching the March of Time. But don't let that faze you—this is good for any season of the year. Note the handbag—a creation by Goody and Mess." (Sew old calendar pages all over plain dress. Make hat from same and jewelry out of real dates. The purse is a box of dates.)

10. "No fashion revue is complete without the traditional bridal gown and the bride's maid or matron of honor. Something old—that's the bride. Something new—that's the ball and chain. Something borrowed—the cookbook she's carrying (boy does she need it!). Something blue—that's the groom's face as he's pushed toward the altar. The duty of the maid of honor is to assist the bride; so she's equipped with the things she really needs—the bucket-shaped headdress, the jewel of a brush (by Fuller) at the waist, and the earrings by Ivory. Also the lovely bridal bouquet by Chore Girl." (Long formal lace curtain for veil, carry ball and chain and cookbook. Use imagination and be just offbeat on a traditional bridal gown.) (MAID OF HONOR—Long black dress. Carry brush with a bouquet made by fastening steel wool on a doily. Make hat from bucket and carry brush in one hand. Small bars of Ivory soap for earrings.)

"And this, friends, completes our little revue, which we hope you have found enjoyable and profitable. Credit for the makeup must go to the Marietta Paint Co. All hairstyles were by Gorgeous George—smiles by Liberace. Now I see that our chauffeurs are waiting in their crisp white coats to take us back to that lively place where we all live—that place with the high walls around it. Goodnight to one and all!"

Ribs, Fig Leaves, and Apples

(a Valentine play)

Setting: Desk, chair, scattered tables and couch, piano, dressing table with teenage items (perfume, nail file, nail polish, powder, mirror, etc.)

Background: Large Bible drawn on paper covering entrance to stage, characters enter stage between pages.

Characters:

Jenny: teenage girl, typically dressed

Eve: woman, dressed in green with large safety pin on skirt, carrying large basket of apples (Note: Whenever Eve isn't talking she's looking . . . inspecting everything in the room, constantly lifting things and trying them.)

Leah: a dowdy, plain woman wearing glasses

Rachel: young woman, pretty, pampered

Gomer: woman, dressed in red (like "street walker") lots of jewelry, dangling earrings, bright red lipstick, carrying a tamborine

Opening: Jenny is seated at the desk with a Bible, open notebook, and pen.

Jenny: This is going to be tough. How can I possibly choose which love story in the Bible to write a song about? (opens the Bible to the first page) "Maybe if I start at the beginning . . ."

(Eve steps out of the large Bible.)

Eve: Love? Did I hear someone mention love? Have I got a love story for you! My Adam . . .

Jenny (interrupting): Who are you? (surprised)

Eve: I'm Eve. Want an apple? (holds out her basket) You wouldn't happen to have an extra fig leaf would you? I was out picking apples in the garden and tore my dress. (looks at pin on skirt) I ought to mend it. Now (pats Jenny on head), you look like a nice Jewish girl.

Jenny: I'm not Jewish.

Eve: You look Jewish . . . anyway, as I was saying . . . what's the matter? You're a little bit young to want to know about love!

Jenny: I have to write a song about the greatest love story in the Bible for my youth group party . . . for Valentine's Day.

Eve: Valentine? What is Valentine?

Jenny: It's a day we set aside to honor love.

Eve: Oh, you worship LOVE? That's not nice, you should only worship God!

Jenny: No, we don't worship it . . . but we . . . well, that is . . . well . . .

(Enter Leah)

Leah: Did I hear you ask about a well? My husband, Jacob, has a lot of wells.

Jenny (to Eve): Who is that?

Eve: Leah, what are you doing here? You should be home minding the children. (aside to Jenny) Such nice boys she has. So . . . Jewish!

Leah: What are you doing here, Eve?

Eve: I'm telling this nice Jewish girl about love . . . you know MY ADAM was the world's *first* lover.

Jenny: I'm *not* Jewish.

Leah (to Eve): Love? Ha, what would you know about love? Why, MY Jacob worked seven years for my father before he married me!

Eve: He meant to marry Rachel, not you, remember?

(Enter Rachel)

Rachel: Oh, there you are, Leah. I was looking for you.

Leah (shrugs shoulders and rolls her eyes): My sister, the "Tag-a-long." I can't do anything by myself without Rachel following along. Ever since she was born I've had to share with her.
(to Jenny) You don't have a sister to share with, you do?

Jenny: Yes (nods . . . begins taking notes)

Leah: Well, don't ever date the same man she does . . . look what happened to us! (points to Rachel and herself)

Rachel: If you're referring to my Jacob, you know he was tricked into marrying you. (shakes finger at Leah)
(to Eve) Now, what's going on here?

Eve (points to Jenny): The little one here wants to know about love . . . which one of us has the best love story.

Jenny: I have to write a song . . .

Rachel (to Jenny): Well, dear, if you want a love story, you'd better write down mine. (moves to couch or chair and leans back, dreamily) You know, Jacob met me at the well and it was love at first sight. We were tending our father's sheep and Jacob kissed me right then and there.

Leah: Well, he married me first. (harshly)

Rachel: But he loved *me* best. (forcefully, fighting with Leah)

Eve: Now, girls, settle down. I still think she should sing a song about my Adam.

Rachel (aside to Jenny): Not Adam . . . he didn't even have a choice. Eve was the only one available!

Jenny (looks at Leah and Rachel): Tell me about your family.

Leah: We have 12 sons. (proudly)

Rachel: They aren't all hers; Jacob's favorite son is the one *I* bore.

Jenny (*writing*): . . . 12 sons . . . (*turns a few pages in the Bible*) What about Ruth and Boaz? That's a beautiful love story.

Rachel (*sarcastically*): You call sleeping at some guy's feet beautiful?

Eve: I still think she should tell about how special the relationship is between Adam and me. I mean . . . we even share a rib. Now, that's being close. I mean, which one of you can say Jacob loved you so much he gave up a rib for you?

Jenny (*murmuring, and continues writing*): . . . ribs . . .

Rachel: That's not the kind of love story she wants. She wants romance and tenderness and . . .

(*Enter Gomer*)

Gomer: If it's romance you want, let me tell. (*brashly pushes aside the other women and perches on the edge of the desk*) I know all about men!

Leah: Hello, Gomer. It's been a long time since you traveled back to Genesis to see us.

Rachel: How's Hosea?

Gomer: Hosea's fine. He stayed home . . . I think he's planning to surprise me with a vacation. You know, the kind where just the two of us are alone. Maybe it'll be out in the valley again . . . he's such a romantic!

Jenny: I like romance . . . tell me about yours.

Gomer: Well, if it's men you want to know about, you've asked the right person. Before I was married I was a . . .

Eve (*rushing to cover Jenny's ears*): Gomer! Not in front of the nice Jewish girl!

Jenny: I'm not Jewish! (*gently pushes Eve away*)

Gomer: I mean . . . I was a . . . "lady of the evening." Anyway, my Hosea . . .

Rachel (*to Gomer*): She doesn't want to hear about you. She's going to write about Jacob and me.

Leah (*shoves in front of the others*): You mean Jacob and me!

Eve: Girls! Girls! Now stop it, all of you. There are lots of love stories that we haven't talked about.

Leah (*to Eve*): Like who?

Eve: There's David and Bathsheba.

Rachel: That woman never gets out of the bathtub! Wonder what she'd smell like if she had to tend the sheep like we did?

Gomer: Have you talked about Solomon? Now there's a guy who really had a way with women! I mean, any guy who can handle 3,000 women . . . ! (*starts filing her nails, looks carefully at bottles of perfume and nail polish on dresser*)

Leah: Three thousand? And I thought it was bad sharing Jacob with my sister! How could he even remember who they were?

Rachel: Humph! He probably just called them by their numbers. You know . . . "number 2,483, come here." I'm glad Jacob isn't like that!

Eve: Hush now, you sound like a bunch of market women, the way you gossip. There are others who might fit the love story she needs. Have any of you seen Esther lately?

Eve (*to Jenny*): Now there's a nice Jewish girl for you . . . and she married a king!

Leah: I stopped by the palace yesterday, but she was cooking . . . you know how that king of hers likes to eat.

Rachel: I'm glad I don't have to prepare a banquet every time I want to see Jacob.

Jenny (*standing up*): There . . . I'm done.

(*they all crowd around her eagerly*)

All: Who did you write about? Was it me? Sing it for us.

Jenny: You can all help me sing it.

(*Music begins, see footnote**)
(*Gomer picks up the beat with her tamborine*)

Verse one:
(*solo by Jenny*)
A little home. A loving man. A place where we can fall in love. It's all I want, all I need, all I ever dreamed would be. I wonder who I'll love . . . and will he love me? This is my love story.
But God is wise and He had planned
This little plan, so here I stand, a teenage girl
questioning my friends about love.

Chorus one: (*all*)
Eve and Leah, Rachel, Gomer
all have told their story and I believe
they will guide and give me wisdom
teach me what it means
to be in love.

Verse two: (*Jenny, solo*)
Three thousand women
cannot tell, the man I'll love
and serve so well
about my love, all my love.
All I ever hope to do
is love a quiet man, raise a family, not making history.
But now I know there's more than that
to love and life. So here I stand
a teenage girl . . . wondering about love and life.

(*Second chorus is in two parts. Eve and Jenny sing the first part using the words to chorus two. Leah, Rachel, and Gomer sing the counter part using the words to chorus one.*)

Chorus two:

It takes ribs, fig leaves, and apples,
bubble bath and banquets . . . all the time,
to keep up with all the women
who would want to try to steal my man.

(End with the words . . . "I will love him. I will love him."
As the song ends they drift off stage one by one with Eve
being the last to leave. When they are gone, Jenny walks
slowly back to the desk, folds her arms, and lays her
head down as though going to sleep.)

* * *

*Note: "I Will Love Him" from the cantata, "The Glory
of Christmas," written by Jimmy and Carol Owens, pub-
lished by Lexicon Music, Inc., and distributed by Word,
Inc., Waco, TX 76703.
This song has a decidedly Jewish beat and fits well with
the theme.

Contributed by
Marcia L. Mitchell
Walla Walla, Washington

Mothers
The Reigning Queen

(to the mother with an 18-year-old son)
Standard Magazine

In stores, on streets, in church, at tea,
The high school girls all speak to me.
I'm greeted with a bright "Hello"
From those I do not even know.
Some other mothers are ignored
    Not me,
I'm practically adored,
    What makes me
Such a reigning queen?
I have a handsome son, 18.

"Mother"

MOTHER SINGS TO DAUGHTER . . .

M is for the migraines that you gave me—
O is for the oceans that I cried
T is for the times your nose was runny
H is for my hair you made go white
E is every curfew ever broken
R is always rushing here and there
All these things together make a mother;
    wish sometimes she had a spare.

DAUGHTER SINGS TO MOTHER . . .

M is for the million things she gave me;
O means only that she's growing old.
T is for the tears she shed to save me;
H is for her heart as pure as gold.
E means everything she's done to help me;
R means right and right she'll always be,
Put them all together they spell Mother,
    a word that means the world to me.

"The Ideal Mother"
otherwise known as "Supermom"

    Each morning she rises long before any other
members of her household. She prepares a
_____ breakfast for her family, which she
    adj.
always serves elegantly using the finest
_____ . When she is sure that each member
    noun
of her _____ family has had a
    adj.
_____ night's rest, she awakens them cheer-
    adj.
fully to the tune of _____ .
                   name of song
The "ideal mother" never nags her family or
_____ them to make sure they are on time.
    verb
But, instead, she _____ reminds them of
            adverb
their morning schedules and sees them off at the door
with a hug and a _____ .
            noun
    The "ideal mom" busies herself throughout the
day with tasks that will add warmth and
_____ to the atmosphere of her home. She
    noun
makes sure that all of her family's clothes have been
properly washed and _____ . She dusts and
                   verb
_____ each room of the house until it
    verb
_____ with every _____ in its
    adj.   *noun*
proper place.
    Our Supermom spends time working outdoors in
her garden, planting _____ and
                     noun
_____ . She tends to the garden daily, mak-
    noun
ing sure all the weeds are _____ and thrown
                     verb
away. She always picks a _____ bouquet of
                     adj.

_____ to add a touch of beauty to the dining
   noun

room _____.
       noun

    The ideal mother never forgets that she must

take _____ care of herself too. She has a
     adj.

daily routine of vigorous _____, which in-
               noun

cludes jogging _____ times around the block.
        number

    When the children arrive home from school, she

greets them _____ with milk and
          adverb

_____. She listens _____ as they
  food   *adverb*

tell her about their _____ day. She
               adj.

_____ them with their homework and drives
  verb

them to their _____ lessons and
           noun

_____ practice.
  noun

    Of course the evening meal is always prepared

_____ and _____ and is an experi-
  adverb   *adverb*

ence in gourmet _____ (ing) for everyone
             verb

present.

    Supermom leaves the kitchen _____
                        adj.

clean and spends the remainder of the evening visiting

and _____ (ing) with her _____ fam-
    verb   *adj.*

ily.

    When the day draws to a close and the little

ones have been _____ into their
           verb

_____, Supermom calls out _____,
  noun   *adverb*

_____, _____,
 greeting   *teen in room*

_____, _____,
 greeting   *teen in room*

_____, _____
 greeting   *college student in room*

The End

A Little Parable for Mother

A young mother set her foot on the path of life. "Is the way long?" she asked. Her guide said, "Yes, and the way is hard and you will be old before you reach the end of it. But the end will be better than the beginning."

But the young mother was full of joy and happiness, and she would not believe that anything could be better than these years. So she romped and played with her children along the way. They enjoyed life together; the sun shone on them; life was; and the young mother said, "Nothing can ever be better than this."

Then night came, and a storm, and the path was dark. The children shook with fear and cold, and the mother drew them close and covered them with her coat of protection; and the children said, "Oh, Mother, we are not afraid, for you are near and no harm can come." And the mother said, "This is better than the brightness of day, for I have taught my children courage and trust in God."

The morning came and there was a hill ahead. The children climbed and grew tired and the mother was tired, but at all times she said to her children, "A little patience and we are there." So the children climbed and when they reached the top they said, "We could not have done it without you, Mother." And the mother walked out into the night, looked up to the stars, and said: "This is better than the last day, for my children have learned fortitude and patience in the face of hardness. Yesterday, I gave them courage and faith. Today, I have given them strength."

The next day strange clouds came, darkening the earth with clouds of war and hate and evil, and the children groped and stumbled and the mother said: "Look up. Lift your eyes to the light." And the children looked and saw above the clouds an Everlasting Glory, and it guided them and brought them beyond the darkness. And that night the mother said, "This is the best day of all, for I have shown my children God."

And the days went on, and the weeks and the months and the years and the mother grew old, a little stooped and gray. But her children were tall and strong and they walked with courage; when the way was hard they helped their mother and when the way was rough they lifted her up. At last a golden gate flung open wide and the mother said, "I have reached the end of my journey. Now I know that the end is better than the beginning, for my children can walk alone and their children after them."

And the children said, "You will always walk with us, Mother, even when you have gone through the gate." They stood and watched her as she went alone and the gate closed after her. They said, "We cannot see her, but she is with us still. A mother like ours is more than a memory—she is a living presence."

(Paraphrased from Temple Bailey's "Parable on Mothers" by Mrs. Lottie Snyder.)

To His Mother

Mother-in-law they say, and yet,
Somehow I simply can't forget
'Twas you who watched his baby ways,
Who taught him his first hymn of praise,
Who smiled on him with loving pride
When he first toddled by your side.
Mother-in-law but, oh, 'twas you
Who taught him to be kind and true.
When he was tired, almost asleep,
'Twas to your arms he used to creep,
And when he bruised his tiny knee,
'Twas you who kissed it tenderly.
Mother-in-law they say, and yet,
Somehow I never shall forget
How very much I owe
To you, who taught him how to grow,
You trained your son to look above,
You made of him the man I love,
And so I think of that today,
Ah! Then with thankful heart I'll say
Our Mother.

What Is a Daughter?

Daughters come in all sizes—
    small, medium, and large—
and every one is wonderful!
A daughter is a combination of all things feminine—
    a collector of clothes, a lover of jewelry, scented
bubble baths, and make-up . . .
    a keeper of secrets and a giver of happiness.
Gentle, clever, full of curiosity,
    bubbling over with irrespressible high spirits,
she has in her nature something of all the great
    ladies of history.
She keeps her parents in pace with the world,
    and her every success is a big moment for them.
No matter how grown-up she gets . . . she'll always be
    younger than springtime to those who love her best.

Proverbs 31:10-31

A Paraphrase from the NIV
by Lynn Deakins

Proverbs 31:10-31

10. A wife who tries hard to have noble character is not easy to find. She is worth far more than rubies, but few ever notice it.
11. Her husband has full confidence in her good intentions and lacks nothing of real value, even if his underwear is still in the dryer as he stands shivering before the dresser.
12. She endeavors to bring him good things, not harm, all the days of her life and occasional nights.
13. She selects wool and polyester and works with tired hands.
14. She is like a merchant ship—even though she tries so hard to diet. She brings her food from supermarkets.
15. She gets up while it is still dark and *is* the servant girl who portions breakfast for her family.
16. She considers a part-time job, pursues it, and out of her earnings stocks up when the case goods sale is on.
17. She sets about her work vigorously—her arms are strong for her tasks.
18. She sees that her job, while profitable, keeps her up doing housework all night long.
19. In her hand she holds a needle and thread to tackle an endless pile of mending.
20. She opens her arms to the poor and needy children of the neighborhood whose moms work full time.
21. When it snows she has no fear for her household, for they are clothed in coats she bought last fall at the Sears sale.
22. If she had time she'd sew a bedspread for her bed; she is clothed in the nicest clothes she can afford.
23. Her husband is respected in the school district where he takes his seat in his office.
24. If she had time to make clothes, she could *never* sell them—she'd rather the merchants supplied the clothing.
25. She is clothed with good intentions, a pure heart, and often laughs at the way her days go.
26. She tries to speak with wisdom—and faithful instruction is usually interpreted as nagging.
27. She watches over the affairs of her household and tries not to eat chocolate cake while watching TV.
28. Her children arise at 6:30 a.m. and howl for breakfast, her husband also, and he praises her if it's french toast rather than Cheerios.
29. Many women *do* noble things, but I can't seem to get organized.
30. Charm is useful and beauty is desirable, but a woman who loves the Lord and tries hard will *surely, someday* be praised.
31. Give her the reward she has earned, and let it be said at the funeral gate—"She really tried hard to be a wife of noble character."

The Padded Cross

Well, here I am, Lord. You said, "Take up your cross," and I'm here to do it. It's not easy, you know, this self-denial thing. I mean to go through with it though—yes sir. I'll bet You wish more people were willing to be disciples like me. I've counted the cost and surrendered my life, and it's not an easy road.

You mind if I look over these crosses? I'd kind of like a new one. I'm not fussy, You understand, but a disciple has to be relevant these days. I was wondering—are there any that are vinyl padded? I am thinking of attracting others, see? And if I could show them a comfortable cross, I'm sure I could win a lot more.

And I need something durable so I can treasure it always. Oh, is there one that's sort of flat so it would fit under my coat? One shouldn't be too obvious.

Funny, there doesn't seem to be much choice here—just that coarse, rough wood. I mean, that would hurt. Don't You have something more distinctive, Lord? I can tell You right now, none of my friends are going to be impressed by this shoddy workmanship. They'll think I'm a nut or something. And my family will be just mortified. What's that? It's either one of these or forget the whole thing? But, Lord, I want to be Your disciple. I mean, just being with You, that's all that counts; but life has to have a balance, too. But You don't understand—nobody lives that way today. Who's going to be attracted by this self-denial bit? I mean, I want to; but let's not overdo it. Start getting radical like this, and they'll have me off to the funny farm. Know what I mean?

I mean, being a disciple is challenging and exciting and I want to do it; but I do have some rights, You know. Now let's see—no blood, OK? I just can't stand the thought of that, Lord . . . Lord? Jesus? Now where do you suppose He went?

Prayers

"More things are wrought by prayer than this world dreams of" wrote Alfred L. Tennyson. Prayer is the language of the soul; prayer spans time and space. And, many times when your heart becomes lighter and your spirit is lifted, someone has touched God and prayed for you.

Test Prayer
from Ann Landers

Now I lay me down to study
I pray the Lord I won't go nutty,
If I should fail to learn this junk,
I pray the Lord I will not flunk.
But if I do, don't pity me at all,
Just lay my bones down in the
    study hall;

Tell my teacher I did my best,
Then pile my books upon my chest.
Now I lay me down to rest
And pray I'll pass tomorrow's test.
If I should die before I wake,
That's one less test I'll have to
    take.[5]

A Prayer for Parents
(you could substitute mothers)
from Ann Landers

O God, make me a better parent. Help me to understand my children, to listen patiently to what they have to say and to respond to their questions kindly. Keep me from interrupting and contradicting them. Make me as courteous to them as I would have them be to me.

Give me the courage to confess my sins against my children and ask them for forgiveness when I know I have done wrong.

May I not vainly hurt the feelings of my children. Forbid that I should laugh at their mistakes, or resort to shame and ridicule as punishment.

Reduce the meanness in me. May I cease to nag; and when I am out of sorts, help me, O Lord, to hold my tongue. Blind me to the little errors of my children and help me to see the good things they do. Give me a ready word for honest praise.

Help me treat my children as those of their own age. Let me not expect from them the judgment of adults. Allow me not to rob them of the opportunity to wait upon themselves, to think, to choose, and to make their own decisions.

Forbid that I should ever punish them for my selfish satisfaction. May I grant them all their wishes that are reasonable and have the courage always to withhold a privilege which I know will do them harm.

Make me fair and just, considerate and companionable, so they will have genuine esteem for me. Fit me to be loved and imitated by my children. O God, do give me calm and poise and self-control.[6]

If Jesus Came to Your House

Lois Blanchard Eades

If Jesus came to your house to spend a day or two—
If He came unexpectedly, I wonder what you'd do.

Oh, I know you'd give your nicest room to such an honored Guest,
And all the food you'd serve Him would be the very best,
And you would keep assuring Him you're glad to have Him there—
That serving Him in your own home is joy beyond compare.

But—when you saw Him coming, would you meet Him at the door
With arms outstretched in welcome to your heav'nly visitor?
Or would you have to change your clothes before you let Him in.
Or hide some magazines and put the Bible where they'd been?

Would you turn off the radio and hope He hadn't heard
And wish you hadn't uttered that last loud, hasty word?
Would you hide your worldly music and put some hymn books out?
Could you let Jesus walk right in, or would you rush about?

And I wonder—if the Saviour spent a day or two with you.
Would you go right on doing all the things you always do?
Would you keep right on saying all the things you always say?
Would life for you continue as it does from day to day?

Would your family conversation keep up its usual pace,
And would you find it hard each meal to say a table grace?
Would you sing the songs you always sing and read the books you read
And let Him know the things on which your mind and spirit feed?

Would you take Jesus with you ev'rywhere you'd planned to go,
Or would you maybe change your plans for just a day or so?
Would you be glad to have Him meet your very closest friends,
Or would you hope they'd stay away until His visit ends?

Would you be glad to have Him stay forever on and on?
Or would you sigh with great relief when He at last was gone?
It might be interesting to know the things that you would do
If Jesus Christ in person came to spend some time with you.

An Evening Prayer

G. Maude Battersby

If I have wounded any soul today,
If I have caused one foot to go astray,
If I have walked in my own willful way—
    Dear Lord, forgive!

If I have uttered idle words or vain,
If I have turned aside from want or pain
Lest I, myself, should suffer through the strain—
    Dear Lord, forgive!

If I have craved for joys that are not mine,
If I have let my wayward heart repine,
Dwelling on things on earth, not things divine—
    Dear Lord, forgive!

Forgive the sins I have confessed to Thee;
Forgive the secret sins I do not see;
For which I know not, Father, teach Thou me—
    Help me to live.[7]

Someone Had Prayed

Grace Noll Crowell

The day was long, the burden I had borne
    Seemed heavier than I could longer bear,
And then it lifted—but I did not know
    Someone had knelt in prayer,

Had taken me to God that very hour.
    And asked the easing of the load, and He
In infinite compassion, had stooped down
    And taken it from me.

We cannot tell how often as we pray
    For some bewildered one, hurt and distressed,
The answer comes—but many times those hearts
    Find sudden peace and rest.

Someone had prayed and Faith, a reaching hand,
    Took hold of God, and brought Him down that day!
So many, many hearts have need of prayer—
    Oh, let us pray.[1]

I Said a Prayer for You Today

I said a prayer for you today
   and know God must have heard;
I felt the answer in my heart
   although He spoke no word!
I didn't ask for wealth or fame
   (I knew you wouldn't mind);
I asked Him to send treasures
   of a far more lasting kind!
I asked that He'd be near you
   at the start of each new day.
To grant you health and blessings
   and friends to share your way!
I asked for happiness for you
   in all things great and small
But it was for His loving care
   I prayed the most of all!

The Housewife

Catherine Cate Coblentz

Jesus, teach me how to be
Proud of my simplicity.

Sweep the floors, wash the clothes,
Gather for each vase a rose.

Iron and mend a tiny frock
Taking notice of the clock,

Always having time kept free
For childish questions asked of me.

Grant me wisdom Mary had
When she taught her little Lad.[2]

The Teacher

Leslie Pinckney Hill

Lord, who am I to teach the way
To little children day by day,
So prone myself to go astray?

I teach them knowledge, but I know
How faint the flicker and how low
The candles of my knowledge glow.

I teach them power to will and do
But only now to learn anew
My own great weakness through and through.

I teach them love for all mankind
And all God's creatures, but I find
My love comes lagging far behind.

Lord, if their guide I still must be,
Oh, let the little children see
The teacher leaning hard on Thee.[3]

Jis' Blue

Etta Oldham

"Jis' blue, God
Jis' blue.
Ain't prayin' exactly jis' now, tear-blind, I guess,
Can't see my way through.
You know those things
I ast for so many times—
Maybe I hadn't orter repeated like the Pharisees do;
But I ain't stood in no marketplace;
It's jis' 'tween me and You.
And You said, 'Ast' . . .
Somehow I ain't astin' now and I hardly know
   what to do.
Hope jis' sorter left, but Faith's still here—
Faith ain't gone, too.
I know how 'tis—a thousand years
Is as a single day with You;
And I ain't meanin' to tempt You with 'If You be . . .'
And I ain't doubtin' You.
But I ain't prayin' tonight, God,
Jis' blue."[4]

COMMUNION SERVICES

A. Traditional
   1. Read 1 Cor. 11:23-32
   2. Communion Song
   3. Table Hostesses:

   Read: *And when the hour was come, he sat down, and the twelve apostles with him. And he said unto them, With desire I have desired to eat this passover with you before I suffer: For I say unto you, I will not any more eat thereof, until it be fulfilled in the kingdom of God. . . . And he took bread, and gave thanks, and brake it, and gave unto them, saying, This is my body which is given for you: this do in remembrance of me* (Luke 22:14-16, 19).

   After reading, each hostess passes the bread on her table and each person breaks off a bit. While bread is being passed, she says, "This represents Christ's body broken for you." When everyone is served, eat the bread together.

   After taking the bread, read: *Likewise also the cup after supper, saying, This cup is the new* testament in my blood, which is shed for you. . . . Take this, and divide it among yourselves: for I say unto you, I will not drink of the fruit of the vine, until the kingdom of God shall come (Luke 22:20, 17-18).

Take a goblet of grape juice and sip it. Wipe the rim with a napkin and hand the goblet and napkin to the person on your left. While the goblet is being passed, the hostess says: "This represents Christ's blood shed for you."

4. When goblet has gone around the table, share some prayer requests, and pray about them.

5. Emcee reads: "And when they had sung a hymn, they went out into the mount of Olives." Sing a reverent song to close.

B. Agape Love Feast

LEADER: In biblical days bread was the principle article of food, while meat, vegetables, or liquid only supplemented the meal. To invite the stranger to share the bread of the household was, and still is, the greatest sign of hospitality. Breaking bread together is the standard method of establishing ties of kinship. Indeed, our English word *companion* means "one who shares bread." As we break bread, we affirm the bonds of friendship that bind us together.

ALL: Now as they were eating, Jesus took some bread, and when He had said the blessing, He broke it, and gave it to the disciples. "Take it and eat," He said. "This is my body and I am the bread of life. He who comes to me will never be hungry."

LEADER: "And it came to pass, as he sat at meat with them, he took bread, and blessed it, and brake, and gave to them and they said one to another, did not our hearts burn within us" (Luke 24:30).

SING: "Let Us Break Bread Together"

1. Let us break bread together on our knees;
   Let us break bread together on our knees.
   When I fall on my knees with my face to the rising sun,
   O Lord, have mercy on me.

2. Let us praise God together on our knees;
   Let us praise God together on our knees.
   When I fall on my knees with my face to the rising sun,
   O Lord, have mercy on me.

LEADER: In Exodus we find these words, "I have come to bring you out of that land to a good and broad land, a land flowing with milk and honey . . . I will be with you, and you shall serve God upon this mountain."

SING: "Beulah Land"
O Beulah Land, sweet Beulah Land,
As on thy highest mount I stand,
I look away across the sea,
Where mansions are prepared for me,
And view the shining glory-shore,
My heav'n, my home, forevermore!

LEADER: Remembering these events, let us break bread together, serving one another in love, eating the bread and the honey and drinking the milk. Our agape breakfast is a love feast. Let us ask God's blessing.

PRAYER: (By Leader)

LEADER: While we finish our agape love feast, let us one by one around each table tell what we are thankful for or express our love and appreciation for each other.

SING: "They'll Know We Are Christians by Our Love"

ALL: "Our Father which art in heaven, Hallowed be thy name. Thy kingdom come. Thy will be done in earth, as it is in heaven. Give us this day our daily bread. And forgive us our debts, as we forgive our debtors. And lead us not into temptation, but deliver us from evil: for thine is the kingdom, and the power, and the glory, for ever. Amen.

SING: "Let's Just Praise the Lord"

C. One-on-One

At an appropriate time, give each lady a small roll. She can take her roll to anyone she wishes to "break bread" with, using the opportunity to express love and appreciation to that person.

NOTES

1. Grace Noll Crowell, "Someone Had Prayed," *Christ and the Fine Arts,* by Cynthia Pearl Maus (New York & Evanston: Harper & Row Publishers, 1959), 724.

2. Catherine Cate Coblentz, "The Housewife," *Christ and the Fine Arts,* by Cynthia Pearl Maus (New York & Evanston: Harper & Row Publishers, 1959), 595.

3. Leslie Pinckney Hill, "The Teacher," *Christ and the Fine Arts,* by Cynthia Pearl Maus (New York & Evanston: Harper & Row Publishers, 1959), 632.

4. Etta Oldham, "Jis' Blue," *Christ and the Fine Arts,* by Cynthia Pearl Maus (New York & Evanston: Harper & Row Publishers, 1959), 724.

5. Ann Landers, "Test Prayer," *Idaho Statesman,* June 24, 1978.

6. Ann Landers, "A Prayer for Parents," *Idaho Statesman,* June 24, 1978.

7. G. Maude Battersby, "An Evening Prayer," *Christ and the Fine Arts,* by Cynthia Pearl Maus (New York & Evanston: Harper & Row Publishers, 1959), 721.

4

Outreach Ministries

KOFFEE KLATCH

GIRLS AT LUNCH

PRISON MINISTRY

MOTHER'S DAY OUT

**EVANGELISM AT
SPECIAL EVENTS**

4 Outreach Ministries

Remember: Evangelism is a foremost goal in any women's ministry. You can incorporate it into any special event you wish. But you may also desire to begin ministries specifically for outreach purposes. Following are some programs designed to win people to Jesus Christ.

KOFFEE KLATCH

Appoint one lady to be in charge of calling two or three others when a new family visits the church. She will also call the guest and ask if some ladies can visit her, saying, "We'll bring our own mugs, if you'll make some coffee." The ladies visit, each taking her own coffee mug. As they leave, each one gives her mug to the hostess or newcomer as a continuing reminder of love and concern.

G.A.L. (Girls At Lunch)

All interested ladies (including those who work outside the home) sign up to have lunch with another lady once a month. This can be done on a small commitment card in the Sunday bulletin.

The cards are given to the chairman, and she selects the names of those who will lunch together. The pair can go anytime during the month. Each lady pays her own way. Every month, each lady will be placed with a different person.

Approximately once a quarter, all those involved will have a time together, for example a Saturday morning breakfast, to talk about their experiences and to invite other ladies in the church to join the program. A good rule to give participants is this: Take the initiative and invite your partner. Don't wait for her to call. If you haven't been able to make contact in the first three weeks, tell the chairman.

PRISON MINISTRY

Prison ministry is not typically thought of as a women's program, but it has the potential to be an exciting outreach tool. Gayla Stowe from Denver writes this about her experiences:

Our goal in prison outreach is to minister in Christ's name to the women right where they are—reaching out to as many as we can. We attempt to keep in touch with the needs of the women—

what they hunger for, what they lack in their lives—and we try to effectively meet those needs. Christ loves these women and wants to touch and heal them . . . it's in His name we go.

If you are interested in beginning a prison ministry, a good organization to be affiliated with is Prison Fellowship, founded by Chuck Colson, with headquarters in Washington, D.C. Depending on the prison administration, each ministry will be run differently. For more information in getting started in this ministry, you may write to the following address:

> Prison Fellowship
> Box 40562
> Washington, DC 20016

MOTHER'S DAY OUT (MDO)

Mother's Day Out is a one-day-of-the-week ministry in which the church provides baby-sitting to mothers in the community. It is a valuable ministry for the following reasons.

1. MDO is an outreach to young couples outside the church. As the child learns to enjoy MDO the family will begin to identify with the church. If a need arises in their home, the couple will be more likely to turn to your church for help. If the couple decides to go church shopping, they will probably start with your church.
2. MDO gives several women in your church opportunity for part-time employment.
3. MDO is a growing experience for the children. They are exposed to Christian values in a group setting. They are given a short time of Bible instruction. Unchurched children learn that church is a fun place to be.

How to Begin

1. Get approval from the pastor.
2. Get approval from the church board. (Before you go to the board, have the details worked out. Know approximately how much money the church will have to spend to get started. MDO should pay for itself on a week-to-week basis. However, if the classes don't fill right away, see if the board is willing to pay the difference.)
3. Appoint a director of Mother's Day Out.
4. Determine the number of classes, children, and workers in your Mother's Day Out. (Don't start too big. You can always grow.)
5. Hire the staff. The director should hire from your church people if possible. Each staff member must be a Christian woman who loves children and who will represent your church well. Line up one substitute.
6. Determine which rooms you will use, and purchase needed equipment and material. If you don't plan to have more children in MDO than in Sunday School, you shouldn't need to buy anything extra. Ask church members for donations of toys, puzzles, books, records, etc.

7. Set a date to begin.
8. Publicize MDO in your church publications. Be sure to include that MDO is open to the public. Encourage your church members to spread the word. Personal contact is your best means of outreach. Run an ad in the local paper.
9. Enroll children. In the beginning, take only standing reservations. Explain to the mother that you will be expecting her to bring her children each week. If she can't come, she should call and let you know in advance. When the classes are full, start a waiting list. If you have a cancellation, call the first name on the waiting list. When your waiting list gets too long, consider beginning another class or adding a worker to a class.

Structure for Mother's Day Out

Below is the structure for an average-sized MDO. It will help you proportion the children and workers.

Baby Room—Birth to about 15 months
        2 workers
        10 babies
Toddler Room—one- and two-year-olds
        1 worker
        8 children
Preschool Room—three-, four-, and five-year-olds
        1 worker
        11 children

This totals 29 children and 4 workers. If 15 of these children are the only child in a family, then they will pay a total of $45.00. (You charge $3.00 per day for mothers with one child.) If 14 of these belong to a two-child family, then they pay a total of $35.00. (You charge $5.00 for mothers with two children.) $45.00 plus $35.00 equals $80.00. Pay your four workers $20.00 each and MDO will break even.

Daily Schedule for Older Children

Below is a suggested schedule of activities during the day for older children. It would be impossible and impractical to try to write a schedule for the toddlers and baby classes.

  9:00—Children begin arriving. Free play with toys in room.
10:00—Most children have arrived by this time. Have a story, film-strip, sing songs, etc.
10:30—Snacks
10:45—Play some organized games. Try to change the setting if possible by going outside, to the gym, or to the Fellowship Hall.
11:30—Lunch
12:30—Nap time
  2:00—(or as soon as child wakes up) Activity time (Color sheets or some simple take-home craft.)
  2:45—Clean up time
  3:00—Everyone goes home.

Tips for Having a Successful MDO

1. Don't organize your classes strictly by the children's ages. Adjust the children according to ability, behavior, and the class size.

2. Sometimes you need to put two children in one family together for the security of the younger child. Always put them in the younger age-group. When the younger child becomes accustomed to his surroundings, the older one can slip out to his age-group.

3. Don't make the mothers feel that they must have the child at the church by 9 a.m. You are never late to MDO. It is better if the children arrive at different times because you can greet each child.

4. Don't serve sugary snacks. Many parents will object and it causes behavior problems. Serve juice or milk and wholesome crackers or fruit. Popcorn is good.

5. Encourage parents to send sensible lunches. They should send easy finger foods that are not messy. Ask them not to include candy.

6. Insist that everyone lie down to rest. Nap time is hard for some children. Have mother bring each child a blanket, towel, or mat. Read to the children or play restful music to help them relax. Partially darken the room. Those children who cannot fall asleep should be allowed to get up and play after 30-45 minutes if they have genuinely tried to rest.

7. Most mothers will come to pick up their children about the same time. Be prepared! Have the children clean up the room about 2:45. You will need a good system for keeping each child's coat, blanket, lunch, papers, etc., together.

The Director

The director is the key person in a successful Mother's Day Out. She should consider this a ministry and not just a program.

After she has accomplished all the items on the "How to begin list," her real ministry begins. She will need to be present each morning as MDO begins to see that the workers are there and everything is ready. She should stay for about the first hour to see that each mother has a copy of the guidelines and has filled out an information sheet (see samples on pages following). The director needs to make an attempt to know each mother and child. As she greets them each week, she can become well acquainted with the family. She should be alert for any opportunity (such as a new baby, a sick child, etc.) for the church to minister to the family.

GUIDELINES FOR MOTHER'S DAY OUT

So that we can properly care for your children, we have set up some guidelines for Mother's Day Out. These guidelines are for the good of the children, the workers, and the facilities. We must ask that everyone comply with these guidelines if they are to use our Mother's Day Out.

1. We charge $3.00 a day for the first child; $2.00 for the second; and $1.00 for the third. If children are picked up before 11:45 a.m. or brought after 12:15 p.m. you will be charged one-half of the rate.

2. The nursery opens at 9 a.m. It closes promptly at 3 p.m. We will charge 5¢ per minute after 3 p.m.

3. Please mark all of your child's belongings, especially bottles and pacifiers.

4. If you have special instructions for the care of your child, please include a note. Nursery workers cannot be expected to remember individual schedules. If there is no note, the attendants will be allowed to use their discretion.

5. We cannot spoon-feed tiny babies. Please put food into an Infa-feeder.

6. We cannot give any medications.

7. If your child has any fever, please leave him at home.

8. Each child who is present at Mother's Day Out between 11:45 a.m. and 12:15 p.m. needs to bring a lunch. Please provide simple finger foods. We provide drinks. We also provide snacks.

9. Each child needs to bring a blanket for nap time. All children will be required to rest for a while in the afternoon.

10. We will observe all school holidays.

These guidelines are made by (director's name). If there are any complaints, questions, or problems, they should be directed to her and not the nursery attendants.

It is a privilege for us to care for your preschool children. We pray that the Lord will enrich their young lives through our Mother's Day Out and that He will bless and renew you during your day out.

SIGN-IN SHEET

CHILD'S NAME	AGE	PHONE NUMBER	AMOUNT PAID

NOTE: The phone number given here ought to be the phone number (or numbers) where you would have the best chance of reaching one of the parents that day. Parents can pay before or after MDO, but be sure they mark down the amount paid at the time they pay.

MOTHER'S DAY OUT

Child's name _____ Birth date _____

Sex _____ Address _____ City _____ Phone _____

Father's name _____ Mother's name _____

Employer _____ Employer _____

Business phone _____ Business phone _____

Marital status of parents: Married _____ Divorced _____ Separated _____

Number of brothers: Older ____ Younger ____ Sisters: Older _____ Younger _____

The family's denominational preference _____

Name of church now attending _____

Does the child attend Sunday School? Regularly _____ Occasionally _____

Has your child had previous experience in day care? _____

Please give any information concerning your child that will be helpful in his experience in Mother's Day Out. (Play, eating, sleeping habits, fears, likes, dislikes, etc.) _____

_____

_____

If your child has any allergies or other medical conditions, please list:

_____

_____

Emergency Contacts—Names and addresses of two family members or friends who can be contacted.

Name _____   Name _____

Address _____   Address _____

Relationship _____ Phone _____   Relationship _____ Phone _____

Name of family doctor or medical facility to call in case of emergency:

_____ Phone _____

I give permission for emergency medical transportation or treatment when I cannot be contacted.

Yes _____ No _____

Parent's Signature: _____ date _____

EVANGELISM AT SPECIAL EVENTS

At the close of your banquet or retreat the emcee may want to offer the ladies an opportunity to accept Christ. You can do this in a number of ways.

One easy way is to ask that any lady desiring spiritual help put an X in the upper right hand corner of her name tag, or on a 3″ x 5″ card that has been given out earlier in the program. Each person gives this to her hostess on the way out or leaves it by her place at the table for the Executive Committee to collect. The cards provide a way to follow up and disciple. Give these names to your pastor also, and you will be coordinating your ministry into the stream of the entire church. Sometimes a more detailed response is appropriate.

At a retreat-type event, distribute the contract shown below and give the ladies an opportunity to complete it. God's plan of salvation is the basis of this contract and needs only an explanation of the four points. Most people have their own methods of developing these, but a simplified presentation is included as supplementary material for these situations.

God has made a place for himself in your heart. He created you with a God-shaped vacuum. God built it and only He can fill it. Let's ask ourselves some questions:

1. Can I become a child of God? Yes. God has made provision. Because of His love for us, He gave us a chance to be reborn.

> *God commendeth his love toward us, in that, while we were yet sinners, Christ died for us* (Rom. 5:8).
> *For God so loved the world, that he gave his only begotten Son, that whosoever believeth in him should not perish, but have everlasting life* (John 3:16).

2. How can I become a child of God? You must personally invite Jesus Christ into your life to forgive your sins and be your Lord. 1 John 1:9 says: *If we confess our sins, he is faithful and just to forgive us our sins, and to cleanse us from all unrighteousness.* John 1:12 adds: *But as many as received him, to them gave he power to become the sons of God, even to them that believe on his name.*

3. How can I know that I am a child of God? He will assure you. His Word says: *God hath given to us eternal life, and this life is in his Son. He that hath the Son hath life; and he that hath not the Son of God hath not life* (1 John 5:11-12).

If you want to be saved, you must make a definite transaction with the living God—based on the Word of God. Do this by praying:

> Dear Lord Jesus, I know that I'm a sinner and need Your forgiveness. I believe that You died for my sins. I want to turn from my sins. I now invite You to come into my heart and life. I trust You as Savior and want to follow and obey You as Lord, in the fellowship of Your Church. Amen.

If you have made the transaction, then as I read aloud, you may sign your "Personal Decision Contract."

4. Now that I am God's child, what do I do next? Confess Him to others. Romans 10:9 says:

> *If thou shalt confess with thy mouth the Lord Jesus, and shalt believe in thine heart that God hath raised him from the dead, thou shalt be saved.*

This will make your commitment complete and will help you gain spiritual strength as you begin to share what Christ is doing in your life. Tell a friend about Jesus. He said, "I am come that [you] might have life, and that [you] might have it more abundantly" (John 10:10).

Being a child of God is exciting!

MY PERSONAL DECISION CONTRACT

Jesus said, "Behold, I stand at the door, and knock: if any man hear my voice, and open the door, I will come in to him, and will sup with him, and he with me" (Rev. 3:20).

GOD'S PLAN FOR ME

    A. God has made provision—He loves me and sent His Son (John 3:16; Rom. 5:8).
    B. How it takes place—by a definite transaction based on the Word of God (1 John 1:9; John 1:12; Rev. 3:20).
    C. Assurance—how can I know for sure? (John 3:36; 1 John 5:11-14).
    D. What do I do now? Confess Him to others (Rom. 10:9).

MY PERSONAL DECISION

Today, _____ at _____ a.m. at _____ Church, I opened my heart and invited Jesus Christ to come in as my personal Savior.

                    Signed _____

I have been confused and didn't know if Christ was living in my heart or not, but I open my heart and receive Christ today, _____ at _____ a.m., at _____ Church—based not on feeling but on the Word of God.

                    Signed _____

I opened my heart to Christ years ago and He is still real today, _____ _____.

                    Signed _____

Appendix

PLANNING CHECKLIST

1. SPECIAL EVENT

2. SPECIAL SPEAKER

3. DATE/TIME

4. PLACE

5. THEME/SCRIPTURE

6. SETTING

   —types of tables

   —podium

   —piano

   —P.A. system

   —colors—tableclothes, napkins

   —estimated number to attend

   —if overnight, make room reservations

7. FOOD—SERVING—CLEANUP

8. TOTAL COST

   —speaker, travel

   —rooms

   —menus

   —decorations

9. FUNDRAISER

10. SELECT

    —hostesses

    —photographer

    —tape recorder person

    —door prizes

11. PROGRAM SCHEDULE

12. DEVOTIONAL

13. SMALL-GROUP INTERACTION/GAMES

14. CENTERPIECE

15. FAVORS

16. PROGRAM COVER

17. NAME TAGS/HOSTESS TAGS

18. SPECIAL FEATURE/ENTERTAINMENT

19. SPECIAL MUSIC

20. REGISTRATION/TREASURER

21. PUBLICITY

22. COORDINATION

23. FOLLOW-UP QUESTIONNAIRE

    —evaluation

    —outreach—letters, visitation

24. NURSERY

Some of these are optional, depending upon your group and the type of event you are planning.

DOORWAYS

DISCOVERIES

LADIES WELCOME

FIRST CHURCH OF THE NAZARENE
Ladies' Ministries Fellowship

"Behold, I have set before
thee an open door."
(Rev. 3:8)

Discover something new, unexpected, and different. Find your possibilities through study, fellowship, and prayer with others. Let us grow and become what God would have us to be.

WEEKLY ACTIVITIES

MONDAY AFTERNOONS—4 to 5 p.m.
  Place: Valley View School
            3555 Milwaukee
  Leader: Molly Pooley
  Study: 3-D (Diet, Discipline, Discipleship)
  Price: $15.00

TUESDAY EVENINGS—7:30 to 9:00 p.m.
  Place: Barbara Johnson home
            5290 Sorrento
  Leader: Connie Brown
  Study: Psalms—Songs of Life by David
            and Sue Burnham.
            Just Living by Faith, a study of
            Habakkuk
  Books: $1.95 each

WEDNESDAY MORNINGS—9 to 10 a.m.
  Place: Fellowship hall at the church
  Leader: Mary Ellen Allen
  Study: 3-D (Diet, Discipline, Discipleship)
  Price: $15.00

THURSDAY MORNINGS—9:30 to 11:30 a.m.
  Place: Fellowship hall at the church
  Leaders: Sandra Forrey
            Roberta Mickelson
  Study: Same as Tuesday evenings (above)
  Books: $1.95 each

THURSDAY NOON
  Place: Prayer and fasting around the church altar with
            Jean Harris and Ruth Boyd

SPECIAL EVENTS

SEPTEMBER 5-6, 1980
        FALL KICK-OFF
  Place: Church fellowship hall
  Speaker: Rubena Poole
  Theme: Doorways and Discoveries

DECEMBER 6, 1980
        LADIES' NIGHT OUT
  Place: Church fellowship hall
  Speaker: Mrs. John Riley—Nampa

JANUARY 10, 1981
        SATURDAY MORNING COFFEE
  Place: Church fellowship hall
  Time: 10 a.m.
  Speaker: Jo Kincade—Nampa

FEBRUARY 14, 1981
        SWEETHEART BANQUET
        (with your sweetheart)
  Place: Fellowship hall
  Speaker: Rev. Chuck Higgins
  Music: Jerry Vevig and Capital Singers

MAY 9, 1981
        MOTHER-DAUGHTER LUNCHEON
  Place: Church fellowship hall
  Speaker: To be announced

JUNE 1, 1981
        LADIES' NIGHT OUT
  Place: Airport Restaurant
  Speaker: Lois Lindbloom—Twin Falls

ACCOUNTABILITY SHEET FOR SPECIAL EVENT

DATE/TIME _____

PLACE _____

SPECIAL EVENT _____

SPECIAL SPEAKER _____

THEME/SCRIPTURE _____

I. *DISCUSSION AND DECISIONS*

1. SETTING—types of tables, podium, piano, P.A. system, colors for tableclothes, napkins, room reservations, if overnight

2. FOOD—MENU

3. TOTAL COST—speaker, travel, menus, decorations, rooms

4. FUNDRAISER

5. SELECT—hostesses, photographer, tape recorder person, door prizes, person to keep photograph book for visual mementos

6. PROGRAM SCHEDULE

7. DEVOTIONAL

8. SMALL-GROUP INTERACTION

9. JOB RESPONSIBILITIES

10. COORDINATION

II. *PLANNING FOLLOW-UP*
—questionnaire
—evaluation sheet
—outreach—letters, visitation

III. *COMMITTEE COMMENTS*
(meeting after event)

JOB RESPONSIBILITY	*PERSON RESPONSIBLE*	*PROGRESS REPORT*	*DATE TO BE COMPLETED*	*ANALYSIS OF EFFECTIVENESS OF EVENT*
1. Centerpiece	_____	_____	_____	_____
2. Favors	_____	_____	_____	_____
3. Program Cover	_____	_____	_____	_____
4. Name Tags/Hostess Tags	_____	_____	_____	_____
5. Special Feature	_____	_____	_____	_____
6. Special Music	_____	_____	_____	_____
7. Registration/Treasurer	_____	_____	_____	_____
8. Publicity	_____	_____	_____	_____
9. Food	_____	_____	_____	_____

MEETING DATE

FOR

PLANNING

Two to six months ahead (or sooner depending upon type of event)

date _____

date _____

date _____

date _____

QUESTIONNAIRE
★★★★*LADIES*★★★★
SIGN UP TODAY

You can find an area of ministry in our fellowship by offering your services. Sunday, January 24, you can sign up for one or several areas of ministry. A *new updated list* is being compiled so we would like *ALL* women to sign up. Sign up in Sunday School class or in the foyer by the bulletin board.

PRAYER CHANGES THINGS (Prayer Chain)

_____ Pray for requests

DO UNTO OTHERS—When someone is ill:

_____ Helping with a meal

_____ Child care

_____ Housework

_____ Housing (traveling groups or speakers)

TENDER LOVING CARE—Helping with:

_____ Baby showers

_____ Wedding showers

_____ Farewells

_____ Funeral dinners

BOUQUETS OF LOVE

_____ Help with decorating for special programs

_____ Showers and seasonal decorating

_____ Silk bouquets available for use

CIRCLE OF LOVE

_____ Available to help widows with transportation or errands

HOSPITALITY

_____ Serving on Kitchen Committee one month a year helping with all-church dinners, cleaning kitchen, etc.

PRECIOUS MOMENTS

_____ I would be interested in teaching a craft I am familiar with

_____ Here are some ideas for craft I would like to see demonstrated

_____   _____

_____   _____

NAME _____

(Sample Questionnaire)

THAT WE MAY INVOLVE ALL WOMEN

We want to better know you—your interests, your desires; so that we might make our ladies' ministries meaningful, active, alive, and alert to the needs of all women.

LADIES' MINISTRIES
BOISE FIRST CHURCH

NAME _____

ADDRESS _____ PHONE _____

Will you please check one or more of the areas below and return to one of the ladies on the Ministries Committee, or leave at the Welcome Center table.

1. *I would like to be involved in:*

    _____ Daytime Ladies' Fellowship

    _____ Evening Bible Study

    _____ Diet, Exercise, and Devotions—Time: _____ 10 a.m. _____ 4 p.m.

2. *I would like to:*

    _____ Lead a diet, exercise group

    _____ Lead a daytime neighborhood Bible Study

    _____ Hostess a daytime neighborhood Bible Study

    _____ Teach a craft class—I am familiar with _____

    _____ Attend a craft class—Here are some crafts I would like to see demonstrated:

    _____   _____   _____

3. *I would like to help with the following ministries:* Special events (Ladies' Night Out, Retreats, etc.):

    _____ theme ideas

    _____ decorations (center)

    _____ artwork

    _____ selling tickets

    _____ publicity, poster, articles

    _____ special feature (skits, music, readings, drama fashions, crafts, etc.)

EVALUATION

1. What needs of yours have been met at retreat so far?

2. Any needs of yours unmet?

3. What did you enjoy most about your small-group times?

4. Any further comments or suggestions?

_____

NAME (optional)

FALL KICK-OFF
EVALUATION

1. What did you like most about the Ladies' Kick-off?

2. What would you like to see changed?

3. What special events would you like to have this year?

4. Would you be interested in an evening fellowship time?

5. Write any suggestions that you have.

_____

NAME (optional)

WOMEN'S MINISTRIES
QUESTIONNAIRE

NAME _____ PHONE _____

ADDRESS _____

AGE-GROUP: 20-35 ____ 35-50 ____ 50- ____ MARRIED ____ SINGLE ____

I work outside the home yes _____ no _____ full time _____ part time _____

I currently serve in the church as _____

Women's Ministries is important to me because:

The greatest need for improvement in Women's Ministries I see is:

I would like to be involved in Women's Ministries in the following areas:

____ Discipleship Classes

     ____ I would open my home for a class

     ____ Daytime is the best time for me

     ____ Evening is the best time for me

     ____ Early morning is the best time for me

____ Craft or Special Interest Classes

     ____ I could lead a class in _____

I would like to be involved in the planning of the following special events:

____ Holiday House Christmas Boutique	____ District Springtime Spectacular
____ Christmas Home Tour	____ Mother-Daughter Luncheon
____ Ladies' Night Out	____ Father-Son Dinner
____ Valentine Banquet	____ Fall Brunch
____ Ladies' Retreat	____ Couples' Retreat

Other facets of Women's Ministries I would like to be involved in are:

____ Publishing Newsletter	____ Wedding Committee
____ Publicity	____ Showers
____ Martha Ministries	____ Funeral Dinners

Additional comments:

FAMILY INFORMATION

Mr. _____

Mrs./Miss _____

ADDRESS _____

CITY _____ ZIP _____

PHONE: Residence _____

       Work (His) _____

       Work (Hers) _____

ANNIVERSARY _____

BIRTHDAYS: (Month & Day)

   Self: _____

   Spouse: _____

   Children: (At Home)

     1. Name _____ Birthday _____

     2. Name _____ Birthday _____

     3. Name _____ Birthday _____

     4. Name _____ Birthday _____

     5. Name _____ Birthday _____

     6. Name _____ Birthday _____

Thank You!

February 4, 1983

Secret Pal Participant:

Thank you for being involved in the Secret Pal program this year. We pray that this will be a meaningful experience as you minister to your sister in the Lord.

The following are some guidelines to help make the Secret Pal experience a positive one for those involved:

      —A card or note each month

      —Prayer support throughout the year, especially if ill or in need

      —A gift remembrance at her birthday, anniversary, and Christmas as a minimum. Additional gifts at other holidays are optional.

The education office near the second level entry is the place to leave items for your Secret Pal or to check for something addressed to you.

If you are not hearing from your Secret Pal please contact your chairman so that she can check into the problem. Also if you are moving or are unable to continue for some reason during the year, give her a call.

The revealing will be scheduled again in January 198__. Have a good year!

MATERIALS REQUIRED
Love, Joy, Peace, Long Suffering,
Gentleness, Goodness, Faith,
Meekness, Temperance   *Gal. 5:22-23*

NOTIONS NEEDED
Forebearance
Elasticity
Variety
Lip Zipper
Sense of Humor
Backbone Stiffening

MEASUREMENTS
How wide is your understanding?
How long is your patience?
How deep is your love?

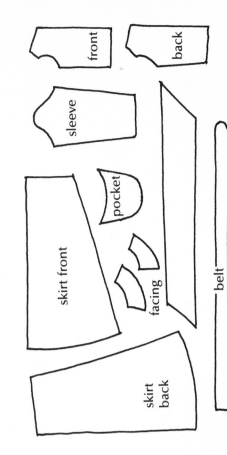

front

back

sleeve

skirt front

pocket

facing

belt

skirt back

"Pattern for Living"

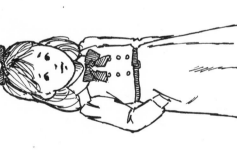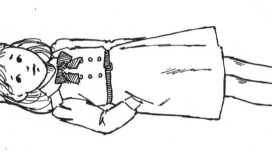

*Mother-Daughter Banquet
May 15, 1982
Church of the Nazarene
Rochester, Indiana*

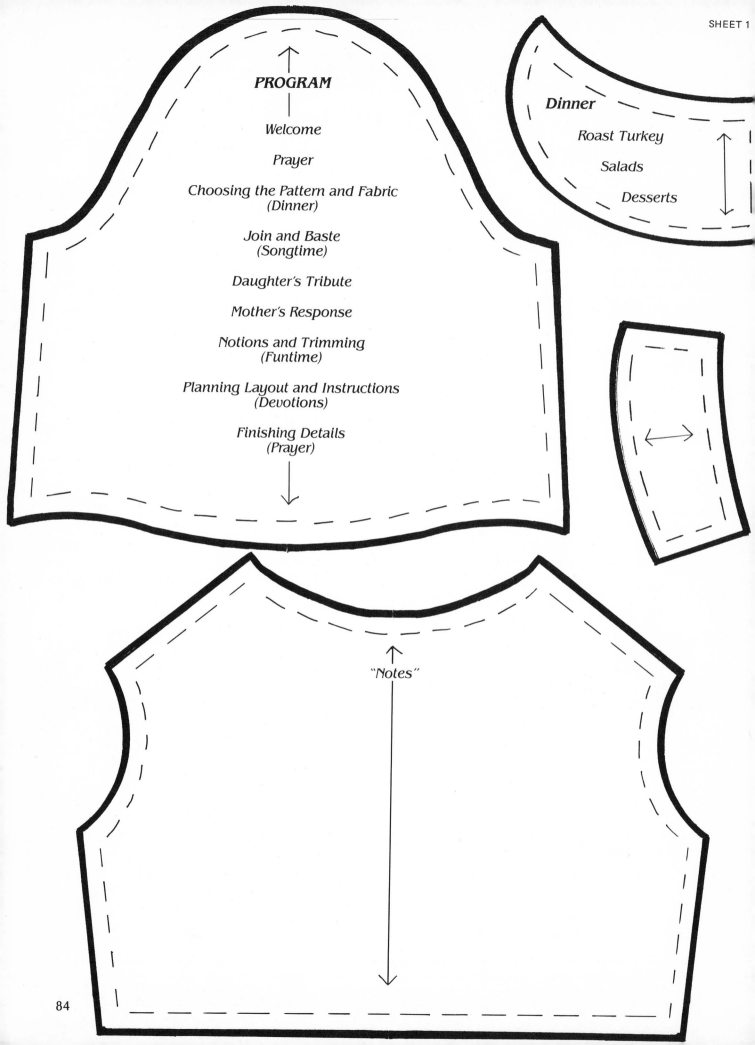

PROGRAM

Welcome

Prayer

Choosing the Pattern and Fabric
(Dinner)

Join and Baste
(Songtime)

Daughter's Tribute

Mother's Response

Notions and Trimming
(Funtime)

Planning Layout and Instructions
(Devotions)

Finishing Details
(Prayer)

Dinner

Roast Turkey

Salads

Desserts

"Notes"

PATTERN
NO. 1974
PARSONAGE QUEEN DOLLS

instruction sheet

This is our annual pattern put out by the Nebraska Pattern Company. It may be used for years with little change in styling. Allow ⅝-inch seam if appetite is average. Add 2 inches for laughing space and ample sleeve room for eating. Lay pattern on the straight of goods so bias pieces will not spoil your finished evening. Cut along specified lines and sew with threads of laughter. Try on finished evening and if results are not satisfactory consult the Nebraska Pattern Company for a complete refund. Satisfaction guaranteed.

> IMPORTANT: "In all thy ways acknowledge him, and he shall direct thy paths."
> Prov. 3:6

> Directions for Doctrine and Life.
> Study Titus 2

STUDY FIRST: "Study to shew thyself approved unto God, a workman that needeth not to be ashamed, rightly dividing the word of truth."
(2 Tim. 2:15)

PLANNING THE LAYOUT: "Let all things be done decently and in order."
(1 Cor. 14:40)

"SEEM" ALLOWANCE: Give others the benefit of the doubt. "Man looketh on the outward appearance, but the Lord looketh on the heart."
(1 Sam. 16:7)

INSTRUCTIONS FOR CUTTING: Cut out all unkind criticism, gossip, fault-finding!

RUFFLING: Don't get ruffled! Not called for in this pattern!

JOIN: In parsonage—keep smiling!

LIP ZIPPER: "Lord, fill my mouth with proper stuff and nudge me when I've said enough."

FACING THE TASK: "In all things shewing thyself a pattern of good works."
(Titus 2:7)

BINDING: See Prov. 6:20-21.

PRESSING: "I press toward the mark for the prize of the high calling of God in Christ Jesus."
(Phil. 3:14)

FINISHING DETAILS: "I have finished my course, I have kept the faith."
(2 Tim. 4:7)

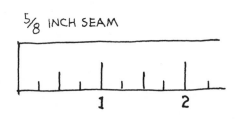

⅝ INCH SEAM

1   2

MAKE DARTS

"Songtime"
"Mother, Mother"
(Tune: Reuben, Reuben)

Mother, mother, I've been thinking
  What a small world this would be
If the dishes, after dinner,
  All like foam, would float to sea.

Daughter, daughter, I've been thinking
  What a great world this would be
If you would be more ambitious
  And do dishes after tea.

Mother, life is such a worry,
  All our clothes keep wearing out.
Stockings run and seams go ripping;
  It's enough to cry about.

Daughter, tears are no assistance,
  You must stop the rip in time;
If you want to know a secret,
  Know, "A stitch in time saves nine."

Mother, why'd you ever marry,
  Drudging day in and day out,
Washing, scrubbing, cooking, mending,
  Family care to fret about?

Daugther, 'Twas because of Teas,
  Like this one we're at tonight,
I just knew you'd need a mother
  For these evenings of delight.

* * * * * * * * * * *

S-M-I-L-E
(Tune: Battle Hymn of the Republic)

Daughters:
  It's wonderful how mothers always S-M-I-L-E
  It's wonderful how mothers always S-M-I-L-E
  If ever you're in trouble,
  It will vanish like a bubble,
  If you tell it all to mother who will S-M-I-L-E

  Chorus:
    Ha, Ha, Ha, Ha, Ha, Ha, Ha, Ha,
    Ha, Ha, Ha, Ha, Ha, Ha, Ha, Ha.

  Mothers:
    It's wonderful how daughters always g-i-ggle-e,
    It's wonderful how daughters always g-i-ggle-e,
    If ever you're in trouble, It will vanish like a bubble,
    If you listen to your daughters when they g-i-ggle.

"Daughter's Things"
(Tune: Clementine)

In the kitchen, in the
  parlor,
In the hall, and on the
  stair,
Daughter's things are
  scattered widely;
You can find them any-
  where.

(Refrain for Mothers)
Oh, my daughter,
  oh my daughter
As a housewife you will
  shine,

(Refrain for Daughters)
'Cause we know you'll
  do it for us
Dreadful sorry,
  Mother mine.

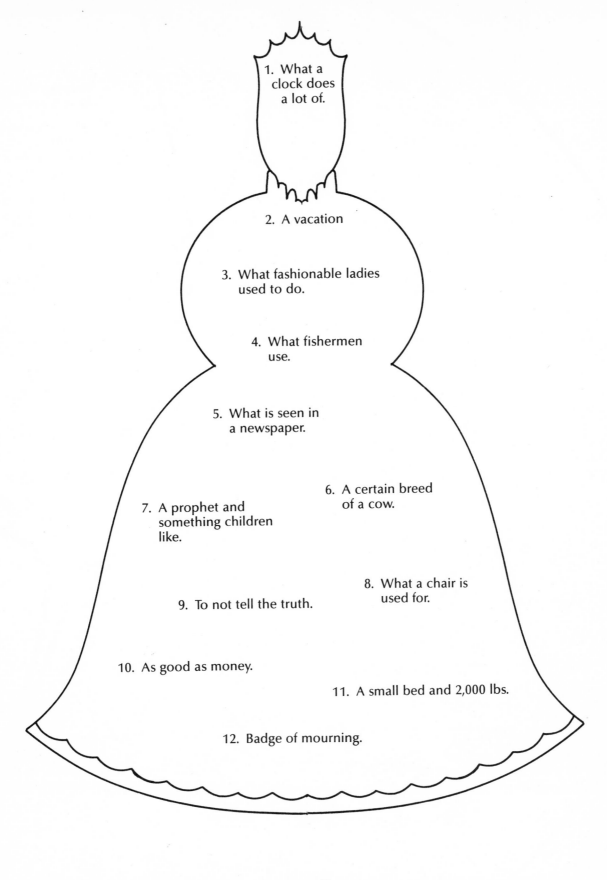

1. What a clock does a lot of.

2. A vacation

3. What fashionable ladies used to do.

4. What fishermen use.

5. What is seen in a newspaper.

6. A certain breed of a cow.

7. A prophet and something children like.

8. What a chair is used for.

9. To not tell the truth.

10. As good as money.

11. A small bed and 2,000 lbs.

12. Badge of mourning.

cut off.

A small envelope containing little pieces of material representing the answers (written in) should be given to each person along with the "lady."

1. ticking	4. net	7. seersucker	10. check
2. outing flannel	5. print	8. satin	11. cotton
3. lace	6. jersey	9. yarn	12. crepe

87